# Table of Contents

Published by Lark Crafts
An Imprint of Sterling Publishing Co., Inc.
387 Park Avenue South, New York, NY 10016

ISBN 978-1-4547-0021-0

First publication in this format 2011.

This material originally appeared as part of
Amigurumi (ISBN 9781600590177).

Text © 2007, Elisabeth A. Doherty
Photography and Illustrations
© 2007, Lark Crafts, an Imprint of Sterling
Publishing Co., Inc.; unless otherwised specified

Distributed in Canada by Sterling Publishing,
c/o Canadian Manda Group, 165 Dufferin
Street Toronto, Ontario, Canada M6K 3H6

Distributed in the United Kingdom by GMC
Distribution Services, Castle Place, 166 High
Street, Lewes, East Sussex, England BN7 1XU

Distributed in Australia by Capricorn Link
(Australia) Pty Ltd., P.O. Box 704, Windsor,
NSW 2756 Australia

Manufactured in China

# Materials & Techniques

Mmm…materials. Let's face it, they're the reason many of us do the crafts we do. Just the other day my mom, who has been doing artwork in pencil for the past few years, came over to my studio and I showed her the new sequins I ordered from an online specialty shop. She oohed and aahed for a few minutes looking at the iridescent flowers and butterflies and finally said, "I think I'm working in the wrong medium." But before you rush off to buy trimmings for amigurumis that don't exist yet, let's talk about the basic supplies you need to make your yarn babies come to life.

## Hooks

Hooks are what make this needlecraft unique, for goodness sake, so we might as well get this portion of our supply list correct. For these amigurumi you'll be working at a very tight gauge. This is a scenario just begging for tired, crampy hands. I urge you to invest the extra few dollars in what are called ergonomic hooks. They have a padded, plastic grip that's much more comfortable than a skinny metal shaft. They're rigid, unlike the completely plastic hooks that will bend all over the place if you try to force them into the very tight fabric you're about to make. They have lovely, smooth anodized aluminum tips that are pointier than most others I have encountered and go in and out of your handiwork without a hitch. Most hobby stores carry these. I discovered these wonderful hooks shortly after beginning my crochet odyssey and am a complete convert. If a regular hook is like a battery-operated, remote-controlled car, an ergonomic hook is like an Italian racing machine.

## Estimating Yarn Amounts

Most of the parts of the amigurumis require only small amounts of yarn. If you have a stash and leftover scrap yarn, you probably won't have to purchase much yarn for these projects. Here are a few tips to help you figure out how much you'll need of each color.

For the small food items and the embellishments on the animals and humanoids, you'll be able to use scrap yarn left over from other projects. The smallest patches of a single color won't take more than 5 or 10 yards (4.6 to 9.1 m) of yarn. And these items are so quick to crochet

that even if you run out of yarn, it's not a big deal to start over. The larger pieces, like the lettuce on the cheeseburger and the pants on the humanoids, won't take more than 25 yards (22.9 m) or so. When you need a color that you don't have in your stash, one ball will be enough to make many small pieces.

For the main color of the animals and humanoids, having one skein of yarn is not a bad idea. In most cases, you'll be able to make a couple of 'gurumis with that skein of yarn.

# Crochet Hook Letter Sizes & Metric Equivalents

There are several different numbering systems for crochet hook sizes, depending upon the material and the manufacturer. The metric system is the only constant measurement scale and is now often included along with the size indicator on each hook.

| Yarn Hooks | | Steel Hooks | |
|---|---|---|---|
| U.S. Size | Metric | U.S. Size | Metric |
| B-1 | 2.25 mm | 00 | 3.50 mm |
| C-2 | 2.75 mm | 0 | 3.25 mm |
| D-3 | 3.25 mm | 1 | 2.75 mm |
| E-4 | 3.50 mm | 2 | 2.25 mm |
| F-5 | 3.75 mm | 3 | 2.10 mm |
| G-6 | 4.00 mm | 4 | 2.00 mm |
| 7 | 4.50 mm | 5 | 1.90 mm |
| H-8 | 5.00 mm | 6 | 1.80 mm |
| I-9 | 5.50 mm | 7 | 1.65 mm |
| J-10 | 6.00 mm | 8 | 1.50 mm |
| K-10 1/2 | 6.50 mm | 9 | 1.40 mm |
| L-11 | 8.00 mm | 10 | 1.30 mm |
| M/N-13 | 9.00 mm | 11 | 1.10 mm |
| N/P-15 | 10.00 mm | 12 | 1.00 mm |
| | | 13 | 0.85 mm |
| | | 14 | 0.75 mm |

## Counting Chain Stitches

As you crochet a chain, it's essential to count the number of stitches you've made. You'll notice that your chain has two distinct sides. The front of the chain—the right side (RS)—should appear as a series of well-defined V-shapes. The wrong side (WS) appears as a series of small bumpy loops. Hold the chain with the right side of the chain stitches facing you. Start counting with the last stitch you completed (not the one on your hook) and don't count the slipknot you made at the beginning of the chain (figure 1).

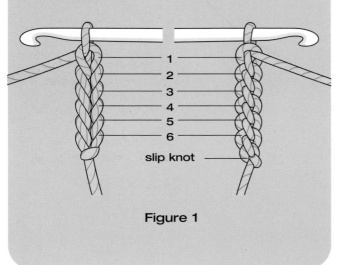

**Figure 1**

## Make Ring

To crochet in the round, you'll need to make a ring (mr) as a foundation for your stitches. (See page 6 for more information on crocheting in rounds.)

**1.** Make a loop by putting the yarn tail behind the yarn coming from the skein, leaving a 4-inch (10 cm) tail (figure 2).

**2.** Use the hook to pull the working yarn through the loop (figure 3)—one loop is now on the hook (figure 4).

After you've made your ring, begin to work the first round as instructed in the pattern. In most cases, you will chain one, then make a number of single crochet stitches into the ring.

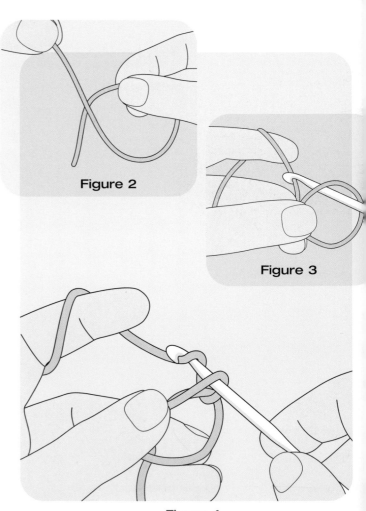

Figure 2

Figure 3

Figure 4

Figure 5

Figure 6

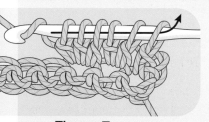

Figure 7

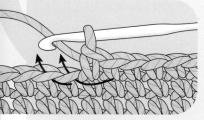

Figure 8

## Bobble

Bobbles are used to make the thumbs and toes on some of the dolls. These instructions are for a basic double crochet bobble. Each pattern that uses a bobble includes instructions for the specific type of bobble used.

**1.** Bring the yarn over the hook and insert the hook into the indicated stitch.

**2.** Yarn over and pull up a loop.

**3.** Yarn over and pull the yarn through 2 loops (figure 5).

**4.** Rep steps 1–4 five more times, working into the same stitch (figure 6). For this bobble, you will have 7 loops on the hook. The number of loops varies depending on the specific type of bobble made.

**5.** Yarn over and pull the yarn through all of the loops on the hook (figure 7). You've completed one bobble. One loop remains on the hook.

## Invisible Decrease

A decrease combines two separate stitches into one stitch. I use an invisible decrease (invdec) most often.

**1.** (Insert the hook into the front loop only of the next st) twice (figure 8).

**2.** Yarn over and pull the yarn through both front loops.

**3.** Yarn and pull the yarn through both loops on the hook.

## Tips for Making Dolls

The following tips will make crocheting the dolls easier.

### Working in Rounds and Spirals

Most of the pieces for the dolls are worked in rounds, not straight rows. (See page 4 for instructions on making a ring to begin crocheting in the round.)

There are three ways to crochet in the round: spirals, joined rounds, and joined, turned rounds.

### *Spirals*

The simplest way to work in the round is to make a continuous spiral. When you come to the end of the round, you just crochet into the first stitch of the previous round and keep going. This works best with single crochet, because the stitches are short enough to create a smooth spiral.

It's helpful to mark the beginning of the round in a spiral with a stitch marker. Otherwise, you won't easily be able to identify where one round begins or ends. The marker can be a locking stitch marker, a length of yarn, or a safety pin. When you get to the end of the round, remove the marker, work the stitch, and replace the marker into the new stitch.

### *Joined Rounds*

Joined rounds are often used when working circular pieces using stitches that are taller than single crochet or in single crochet when the slant caused by the spiral is undesirable.

When working in joined rounds, crochet around the entire piece using the specified stitch. When you reach the end of the round, work a slip stitch into the first stitch of the previous round. Make one or more chains, as directed in the pattern, and begin the next round.

*Note:* I count the chain(s) at the beginning of each round as a stitch.

*Joined, Turned Rounds*

Sometimes when working in joined rounds, you will turn at the end of each round and work back in the opposite direction.

When working in joined, turned rounds, crochet around the entire piece using the specified stitch. When you reach the end of the round, work a slip stitch into the first stitch of the previous round. Turn the piece over, then make one or more chains, as directed in the pattern, and begin the next round, working in the opposite direction than the previous round.

## Counting Rounds and Stitches

Don't assume that counting stitches is something only an amateur would do. Even crochet experts count their stitches. It's the only way to ensure that you're following a pattern exactly. It's a good idea to check your stitch count periodically, especially when the number of stitches in each row or round changes. This may seem like a hassle, but it will save you much frustration in the long run.

You already know how to count chain stitches in a foundation chain (see page 4).

## Counting Rounds

After you work a few rounds of crochet, you'll notice that each round creates a noticeable ridge. Between the rows is an indentation, or valley, that clearly separates the rounds. The valleys are visible in spiral crochet, and in joined rounds. They are less visible in joined, turned rounds.

To count the rounds in a piece of crochet, lay your work on a flat surface. Count the ridges of each crochet round (figure 9).

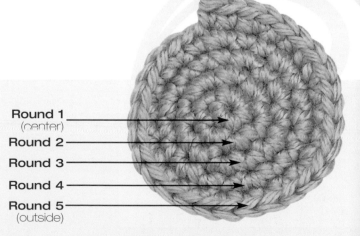

Round 1 (center)
Round 2
Round 3
Round 4
Round 5 (outside)

**Figure 9**

## Counting Stitches

When you look even more closely at a piece of crochet, you'll see that there are several parts to each stitch.

At the top of the stitch is a V. This is where you insert your hook to work another stitch.

Along a row or round of completed stitches you will see that there are posts inside of the valleys. The posts are the vertical parts of the stitches. In between two stitches is a space, which makes up part of the valley. This is where you will insert eye shafts, when instructed in the pattern.

To count the crochet stitches in a completed row, lay your work on a flat surface. Count the vertical part—the post—of each crochet stitch as shown (figure 10).

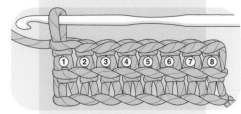

**Figure 10**

## Closing the Hole of Remaining Stitches

When you finish working a piece of circular crochet that forms a 3-D object, you must close the small hole that remains. This is normally completed after stuffing the piece.

**1.** Thread the yarn tail onto a tapestry needle.

**2.** Insert the needle through the front loop of each stitch around the opening (figure 11).

**3.** Pull the tail tight to close the hole (figure 12).

**4.** Weave in the end and clip it close to the surface of the crochet.

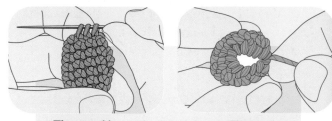

**Figure 11**          **Figure 12**

## Invisible Join

When you finish working a piece of circular crochet that forms a flat circle, you must join the end of the last stitch to the first stitch of the previous round to form an invisible join.

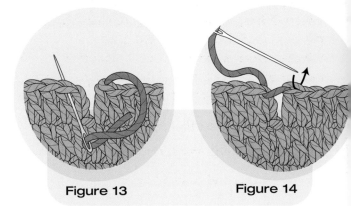

**Figure 13**          **Figure 14**

**1.** Thread the yarn tail onto a tapestry needle.

**2.** Pull the yarn through under the V of the first stitch of the previous round (figure 13).

**3.** Insert the needle into the center of the last stitch on at the end of the last round (figure 14) and pull the yarn through to secure.

**4.** Weave in the end and clip it close to the surface of the crochet.

# Assembling your 'Gurumis

Instructions are given in the patterns telling you to "whipstitch such and such to body using the photo as a guide," and this really is something you will have to get a feel for on your own. I define whipstiching as "sew any which way you can manage it." Some of you may well find this the most difficult part of making the dolls as it lacks the pleasant, rhythmic feel of crocheting. Don't despair; I have confidence that you will soon develop your own tricks and techniques to go along with the ones that I am about to share.

For pinning the ear, limb, tail, or whatever else I am sewing my favorite pins are the large, blunt knitting seaming pins that I mentioned in the materials section. They have heads on them that are big enough not to become lost in the crochet and the rounded tips won't split your stitches.

To do the actual stitching I use either yarn or invisible machine sewing thread. A few general rules of thumb: use yarn and a tapestry needle for pieces that are being sewn onto an area the same color as the pieces themselves or for ones that will receive more wear. Use invisible thread and a regular sewing needle for embellishments or pieces of contrasting color. When working with yarn for sewing, it is important to follow these steps:

**1.** Pull your yarn through the stuffed part of the amigurumi.

**2.** Snake it through some stitches to secure it.

**3.** Sew your pinned piece in place.

**4 and 5.** Secure the yarn again by repeating steps 2 and then 1.

**6.** Fasten off the yarn.

This business of snaking the yarn through some stitches is much like the process of weaving in ends. But in this case, you have three added challenges: working only from the right side, adding the length of yarn in as well as ending it off and making sure it is secure enough it attach a floppy bit.

## Special Techniques

The following techniques go beyond the basics of crochet to give you skills to help make your creations unique and special.

### Twisted Cord

I used a twisted cord to create the stem on the carrot on page 17. Twisted cords also make great belts and other kinds of ties.

**1.** Twist each strand of the cord by itself in a clockwise direction (figure 15). Do not let go, or the strands will untwist!

**2.** Hold all of the strands of the cord together, and let them twist onto each other in a counter clockwise direction (figure 16).

**3.** Tie a knot in the end of the cord to keep it from untwisting. Trim the ends even, if desired.

With the invisible thread, hiding and discreetly securing the thread is not as important. You can simply sew a knot around the post of a stitch from where you choose to start and make another knot where you stop. I do, however, like to hide the ends inside of the stuffing, if possible, because they tend to be a little pokey. While doing the whip stitching, regardless of whether or not I am using yarn or invisible thread, I prefer to go under the posts of the stitches as I feel this is the most inconspicuous, although this is not always feasible. Sometimes improvisation will be your best option.

I know this part of the process might seem like a bit of a drag, where projects tend to get stuck in the UFO (unfinished object) stage. But really that would be a shame, your are so close. The saddest sight in my studio is the "abandoned box" where unassembled doll parts languish; don't let this happen to your creations.

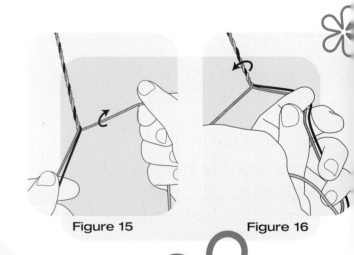

Figure 15        Figure 16

## Stringing Beads onto Yarn

To string beads onto yarn, cut a piece of thread three or four inches (7.6 to 10.2 cm) long, fold it over a piece of yarn, and thread it onto a sewing needle as shown in figure 17. Push the thread through the bead, then pull the yarn through.

If you have trouble stringing your beads onto the yarn with a regular sewing needle, your may prefer using a flexible beading needle with a large eye (figure 18).

Seed beads are irregularly shaped and stringing them can be difficult to do if the holes in your beads are small. It's helpful to look at your beads and try to use the ones that seem to have the largest holes. If all else fails you can sew the beads on after the project is finished.

Although it's simple to remove any unused beads from the yarn after finishing your work, adding them mid-project creates extra labor, so pre-string more beads than you think you'll need.

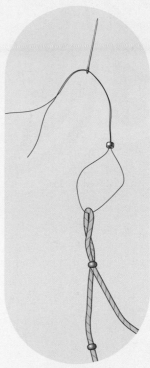

**Figure 17**

## Changing Color (or Yarn)

Crochet might become boring if you were allowed to use only one color or one type of yarn to create a project. And imagine how difficult it would be if you had to use one—and only one—continuous thread to crochet. It would certainly make crochet a less portable craft.

Should you run out of yarn or want to change colors or yarns while you're working, avoid joining with a knot—it's messy and, incredibly, not the most secure way to attach a new piece of yarn.

**1.** Work to the point where there are two loops of the last stitch before the color change remaining on the hook.

**2.** Drop the old color; yarn over and complete the stitch with the new color.

When possible, work over the ends of the color not in use, catching them in the crochet stitches as you work the next round. This will reduce the number of ends to weave in later.

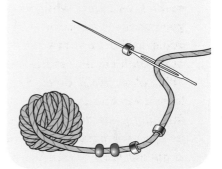

**Figure 18**

## Taking Care of Your Hands

This tight, tight crochet can be tough on your hands. Take a break every now and then to massage and stretch your hands. Here's a testimonial haiku I wrote about the benefits of stretching.

Carpal Tunnel Stung

Wrists Hands Fingers
Ached Numb

Saved by Stretches

# Embroidery Stitches

I use embroidery to add facial expressions and fine details to my projects. You will need an embroidery needle and perle cotton or embroidery floss to work these stitches onto the surface of a crocheted piece. If you've never done embroidery before, you may want to make a gauge circle (page 14), and practice these stitches on it before embroidering on a real project.

## Blanket Stitch

This edging stitch can be decorative, functional, or both. After anchoring the thread near the fabric edge from the wrong side, insert the needle again from the right side so it's perpendicular to the fabric edge. Pass the needle over the thread and pull, repeating for each successive stitch (figure 19).

## Chain Stitch

To make chain stitch, bring the needle up along the stitching line and hold the thread down with one thumb near that spot. Insert the needle right next to the point from which it emerged and bring its tip back out a short distance along the stitching line. Pull the thread through to create a loop, keeping the working thread under the needle's point. Make subsequent loops, or chains, by inserting the needle right next to the point from which it just emerged, again holding the thread down with one thumb near that spot and repeating the previous steps (figure 20).

## Satin Stitch

Satin stitch is composed of parallel rows of straight stitches (figure 21).

## French Knot

French knots are created by wrapping the thread around the needle one, two, or three times, then inserting it back into the fabric at the point where the needle emerged (figure 22).

## Stem Stitch

In stem stitch, the thread always emerges on the left of the previous stitch. Make small, even stitches along the line to follow, sewing from left to right (figure 23).

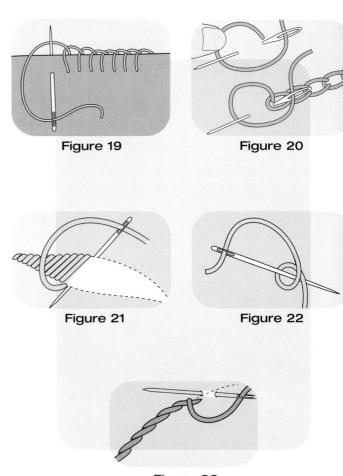

Figure 19

Figure 20

Figure 21

Figure 22

Figure 23

## Abbreviations

This table lists some common crochet abbreviations.
Each pattern also includes a list of stitches and techniques
used, with their abbreviations.

| | |
|---|---|
| () | repeat the instructions in the parentheses the number of times specified |
| * | repeat the instructions after the * as instructed |
| approx | approximately |
| beg | begin(ning) |
| BLO | back loop(s) only |
| ch(s) | chain(s) |
| cm | centimeter(s) |
| dc | double crochet(s) |
| dec | decrease(-ing) |
| FLO | front loop(s) only |
| FPdc | front post double crochet |
| g | gram(s) |
| hdc | half double crochet(s) |
| inc | increase |
| invdec | invisible decrease |
| lp(s) | loop(s) |
| m | meter(s) |
| mr | make ring |
| oz | ounce(s) |
| patt | pattern |
| RS | right side(s) |
| rem | remain(ing) |

| | |
|---|---|
| rep | repeat(ing) |
| rnd(s) | round(s) |
| sc | single crochet(s) |
| sc2tog | single crochet 2 together |
| sk | skip |
| sl st | slip stitch(es) |
| st(s) | stitch(es) |
| tog | together |
| tr | treble crochet(s), (sometimes called triple crochet) |
| WS | wrong side(s) |
| yd | yard(s) |
| YO | yarn over hook |

# Gauge

Common knowledge would have it that gauge is not important when making stuffed toys. When I taught my first amigurumi class I had my students plunge headlong into following the pattern with no regard for gauge, with discouraging results later on. I can hear the groans from the audience already, but the fact is, as with most other knitting and crocheting patterns, gauge is important here as well. While it's true that your finished item need not fit a person's measurements, there are other, equally important reasons to make the simple gauge circle that I have provided instructions for. For one thing, in my experience, crocheters vary greatly in stitch tension. So if I use a 3.5mm/E-4 hook to make my dolls, there's no telling what size you'll need to even come close to achieving similar results.

The reason we want a specific gauge is twofold. Firstly, we want the fabric to stuff firmly and as easily as possible. As I mentioned before, stuffing can be tricky, but it is much easier to do if you take time to get the correct gauge. Stuffing a doll that has been made too loosely is endlessly frustrating. The fabric starts to pull apart and you can see the stuffing from the little holes in between the stitches. Secondly, the embellishments and templates I have provided are sized to a doll that has been made to the proper gauge, so if your doll is way too big or way too small, the eyes and other fancy bits simply will not look right.

The good news is that your gauge does not have to be super precise and you only need to measure it once for the whole book, yea! So following is a pattern for a simple circle. If you make it with a 3.5mm/E-4 hook and it is the size it should be, great. Thereafter, you can use the size hooks suggested throughout the book. But if the circle is too small, go up a hook size until your circle is the right measurement and when a pattern you're working on calls for a hook size other than 3.5mm/E-4, try going up the same amount of sizes that you went up for the gauge circle. Similarly, if your circle is too big, go down a hook size until your circle is the right measurement. When a pattern you're working on calls for a hook size other than 3.5mm/E-4, try going down the same amount of sizes that you went down for the gauge circle.

2"

## Universal Gauge Circle

To make a gauge circle, you will need approx 10yd/9.1m of worsted weight "soft-type" yarn in any color, a 3.5mm/E-4 crochet hook, and a ruler.

*Note:* The Universal Gauge Circle is worked in joined rnds. Ch 1 at beginning of rnds counts as a stitch.

Make a starting ring (see page 4 for instructions).

**Rnd 1:** Ch 1, work 5 sc in ring; join with sl st in first sc; pull starting ring closed—6 sc.

**Rnd 2:** Ch 1, sc in first st, 2 sc in next 5 sts; join with sl st in first sc—12 sc.

**Rnds 3–5:** Ch 1, sc around increasing 6 sc evenly spaced around. Avoid placing increases in the same place every round; join with sl st in first sc—30 sc at end of rnd 5.

Measure across the center of the circle. The diameter of your circle should be approximately 2"/5 cm.

If your circle is too small, try again with a larger hook.

If your circle is too large, try again with a smaller hook.

Although quite similar, these brands of acrylic yarn vary slightly from each other in thickness, as do some colors within each brand. A variation of up to ⅛"/3mm should be OK.

# Not-So-Crunchy Carrot

This is a very straightforward pattern. It's fun to make because of the simple details that make it look realistic. The root is embellished with embroidered lines and the twisted cord stem requires no crochet techniques whatsoever. For those wanting to build their skills for the larger projects at the back of the book, the small circumference of the circle is great practice for making arms for Benny the Monkey (page 55).

## Skill Level

Beginner

## Finished Measurements

Approx 4"/10.2cm long,
    excluding stem

## You Will Need

Worsted weight "soft-type"
    acrylic yarn:
    Color A: orange
    Color B: avocado
*See page 2 for tips on estimating
    yarn amounts.*
Crochet hook:
3.5mm/E-4 or size to obtain gauge
Tapestry needle
Polyester fiberfill
Perle cotton, size 5, dark orange
Embroidery needle

## Gauge

5 rnd gauge circle = 2"/5cm
*See page 14 for instructions on
    making a gauge circle.*

## Stitches and Techniques Used

Make ring (mr), page 4
Single crochet (sc)
Invisible decrease (invdec),
    page 5
Changing colors, page 11

## Instructions

Starting at bottom, with color A, mr.

**Rnd 1:** Ch 1, 4 sc in ring, pull starting ring closed (4 sc).

**Rnds 2 and 3:** Inc 2 sc evenly (8 sc at the end of rnd 3).

**Rnd 4:** Sc in each sc.

**Rnd 5:** Inc 1 sc (9 sc).

**Rnd 6:** Sc in each sc.

**Rnds 7–24:** Rep rnds 5 and 6 nine times (18 sts).

**Rnd 25:** (Invdec, sc in the next st) 6 times (12 sts).

Switch to color B in last st of rnd 25.

**Rnd 26:** (Invdec, sc in the next 2 sts) 3 times (9 sts).

### Finishing

Stuff carrot. Fasten off, leaving an 18"/45.7cm tail. Thread onto tapestry needle. Close the hole as illustrated on page 8. Bring the yarn end up through the center of the hole. Cut an additional 18"/45.7cm length of color B. With tapestry needle, thread it under rnd 26 leaving 9"/22.9cm on either side. Make a twisted cord (see page 10 for instructions) with these three lengths of yarn for the carrot stem. Knot the end of the cord with an overhand knot. If desired, use Perle cotton and an embroidery needle to add chain stitch embroidery on carrot as shown in the photo.

This project was made with 1 skein each of

**Color A: Bernat's Satin (100% acrylic, 3.5oz/100g, 166yd/152m) in #04605, Sunset**

**Color B: Red Heart's Soft (100% acrylic, 5oz/140g, approx 256yd/234m) in #4420, Guacamole**

# Fresh Strawberries

A pint of these life-sized crocheted berries would look sweet displayed in a basket or bowl. The Humanoids like to carry them around as snacks, too. Just sew a loop of elastic onto the back of the berry that's small enough to fit tightly around their little hands.

## Instructions

Starting at bottom, mr.

**Rnd 1:** Ch 1, 4 sc in ring, pull starting ring closed (4 sc).

**Rnd 2:** Inc 2 sc evenly spaced (6 sc).

**Rnd 3:** Inc 3 sc evenly spaced (9 sc).

**Rnd 4:** Sc in each sc.

**Rnds 5 and 6:** Rep rnds 3 and 4 (12 sc at end of rnd 6).

**Rnds 7–10:** Inc 3 sc evenly (24 sc after rnd 10).

**Rnd 11:** Sc in each sc.

**Rnd 12:** (Invdec, sc in the next 2 st) 6 times (18 sts).

**Rnd 13:** (Sc in the next st, invdec) 6 times (12 sts).

**Rnd 14:** (Invdec, sc in the next 2 st) 3 times (9 sts).

## Finishing

Stuff berry. Fasten off, leaving an 18"/45.7cm tail. Thread tail onto tapestry needle. Close hole as illustrated on page 8. Weave in end.

## Strawberry Hull

Cut one star shape out of green felt, using the template on page 63 as a guide.

Using the light green Perle cotton and embroidery needle, work blanket stitch around the edge of the hull. Work a satin-stitch star in the middle of the hull, referring to the photo as a guide. In the middle of the satin-stitched star, embroider one French knot.

Glue the hull to the top of the strawberry using straight pins to keep it in place while it dries.

## Seeds

With invisible thread and beading needle, sew approx 50 seed beads all over the strawberry, spacing them randomly. Try to nestle the beads into the valleys in between the rnds so they look more realistic. (See page 11 for instructions.)

This project was made with 1 skein of
**Red Heart's Soft (100% acrylic, 5oz/140g, approx 256yd/234m) in #5142, Cherry Red**

## Skill Level
Easy

## Finished Measurements
Approx 2"/5.1cm tall by 1¼"/3.2cm wide

## You Will Need
Worsted weight "soft-type" acrylic yarn in red
*See page 2 for tips on estimating yarn amounts.*
Crochet hook:
    3.5mm/E-4 or size to obtain gauge
Polyester fiberfill
Tapestry needle
Wool or wool-blend felt, green
Perle cotton, size 5, light green
Embroidery needle
Craft glue

Straight pins
Invisible thread
Beading needle
50 pale yellow seed beads, size 10
Template, page 63

## Gauge
5 rnd gauge circle = 2"/5cm
*See page 14 for instructions on making a gauge circle.*

## Stitches and Techniques Used
Make ring (mr), page 4
Single crochet (sc)
Invisible decrease (invdec), page 5
Blanket stitch, page 12
Satin stitch, page 12
French knot, page 12

# Sandwich Cookie

Only the grumpiest of grumps wouldn't find a plateful of these tasty treats amusing. Secret: the cookie half is also a darling flower. Make it on its own in fancy yarn scraps for a cute pin or embellishment.

## Instructions

### Cookie (make 2)

*Note:* Cookie is worked in joined rnds. Ch 1 at beginning of rnds counts as a st.

Starting at bottom, with color A, mr.

**Rnd 1:** Ch 1, 5 sc in ring, sl st to first sc to join, pull starting ring closed (6 sc).

**Rnd 2:** Ch 1, sc in the same sp, 2 sc in the next 5 sc, sl st to first sc to join (12 sc).

**Rnd 3:** Ch 1, sc in the same sp, sc in the next st, (2 sc in the next st, sc in the next st) 5 times, sl st to first sc to join (18 cs).

**Rnd 4:** Ch 3, sk the sp you sl st-ed into and the next st, sc in the next st, (ch 2, sk the next st, sc in the next st) 6 times, ch 2, sl st into the first ch of the rnd (9 ch 2 lps).

**Rnd 5:** Ch 1, [(sc 3 hdc sc) in the next ch 2 loop, sk next sc] 9 times.

Fasten off, leaving an 18"/45.7cm tail. Join to first sc of rnd 5 as illustrated on page 8. Weave in ends.

### Crème Filling (make 1)

*Note:* Filling is worked in a continuous spiral. Do not join rnds. You may wish to use a marker to indicate the beginning of the rnd.

Starting at bottom, with color B, mr.

**Rnd 1:** Ch 1, 6 sc in ring, pull starting ring closed (6 sc).

**Rnd 2:** 2 sc in each st (12 sc).

**Rnds 3–6:** Inc 6 sc evenly spaced (36 sc at the end of rnd 6).

**Rnd 7:** Sc in each sc.

**Rnd 8:** (Invdec, sc in the next 4 st) 6 times (30 sts).

**Rnd 9:** Sc in the next 2 sts, (invdec, sc in the next 3 sts) 5 times, invdec, sc in the next st (24 sts).

**Rnd 10:** (Invdec, sc in the next 2 st) 6 times (18 sts).

**Rnd 11:** (Sc in the next st, invdec) 6 times (12 sts).

**Rnd 12:** (Invdec, sc in the next 2 st) 3 times (9 sts).

Fasten off, leaving an 18"/45.7cm tail. Close hole as illustrated on page 8. Weave in end.

### Assembly

Flatten crème filling. Stack cookies on either side of filling with WS facing in. Using the tapestry needle and an 18"/45.7cm length of A, sew all three pieces together through rnd 3 of the cookies; there is no need to sew the petals down. Weave in ends.

This project was made with 1 skein each of

**Color A:** Bernat's Satin (100% acrylic, 3.5oz/100g, 166yd/152m), in #040130, Mocha

**Color B:** Bernat's Satin (100% acrylic, 3.5oz/100g, 166yd/152m), in #04007, Silk

## Skill Level

Easy

## Finished Measurements

Approx 2"/5.1cm diameter

## You Will Need

Worsted weight "soft-type" acrylic yarn:
  Color A: brown
  Color B: off white
*See page 2 for tips on estimating yarn amounts.*
Crochet hook:
  3.5mm/E-4 *or size to obtain gauge*
Tapestry needle

## Gauge

5 rnd gauge circle = 2"/5cm
*See page 14 for instructions on making a gauge circle.*

## Stitches and Techniques Used

Make ring (mr), page 4
Chain (ch)
Single crochet (sc)
Slip stitch (sl st)
Skip (sk)
Half double crochet (hdc)
Invisible decrease
  (invdec), page 5
Repeat (rep)

# Cutecakes

These crocheted confections would make adorable zipper pulls or cell phone charms if you attached a lobster claw clasp to the top. They would also be a welcome addition to any little girl's tea party set.

## Skill Level
Intermediate

## Finished Measurements
Approx 2"/5.1cm tall by 1½"/3.8cm wide

## You Will Need
Worsted weight "soft-type" acrylic yarn:
  Color A: pink
  Color B: chocolate brown
  Color C: lime green
*See page 2 for tips on estimating your amounts.*
Crochet hooks:
  3.5mm/E-4 or *size to obtain gauge*
  3.25mm/D-3
  2.75 mm/C-2
Polyester fiberfill
Tapestry needle
Invisible thread
Beading needle
40 pink seed beads, size 10

## Gauge
5 rnd gauge circle = 2"/5cm
*See page 14 for instructions on making a gauge circle.*

## Stitches and Techniques Used
Make ring (mr), page 4
Single crochet (sc)
Crab stitch (reverse single crochet)
Front Loop Only (FLO)
Back Loop Only (BLO)
Invisible decrease (invdec), page 5
Front Post Double Crochet (FPdc)

## Instructions

### Cutecake Top (make 1)

Starting at icing, with 3.5mm/E-4 hook and color A, mr.

*Note:* Cutecake Top is worked in a continuous spiral. Do not join rnds except as noted. You may wish to use a marker to indicate the beginning of the rnd.

**Rnd 1:** Ch 1, 6 sc in ring, pull starting ring closed (6 sc).

**Rnd 2:** Inc in each sc (12 sc).

**Rnds 3 and 4:** Inc 3 sc evenly spaced (18 sc at the end of rnd 4).

**Rnd 5:** Sc in each sc.

**Rnd 6:** Sc in each sc. Join to second sc in rnd with a sl st. Ch 1. Do not turn.

**Rnd 7:** Work crab stitch in FLO. Fasten off color A. Weave in end.

**Rnd 8:** Attach color B in any back loop. Working in BLO, sc in each st. Do not join.

**Rnd 9:** Sc in each st, working through both loops.

**Rnd 10:** Invdec 9 times (9 sts).

Stuff cutecake top.

Fasten off, leaving an 18"/45.7cm tail. Thread tail onto tapestry needle. Close hole as illustrated on page 8. Weave in end.

## Paper (make 1)

Starting at bottom, with 3.25mm/D-3 hook and color C, mr.

*Note:* Paper is worked in joined rnds. Starting ch at beginning of rnds counts as a stitch.

**Rnd 1:** Ch 1, 5 sc in ring, join with sl st in first sc, pull starting ring closed (6 sc).

**Rnd 2:** Ch 1, sc in same sc as join, 2 sc in next 5 st join with sl st in first sc (12 sc).

Switch to 2.75mm/C-2 hook.

**Rnd 3:** Ch 3, dc in each st, join with sl st in first dc.

**Rnds 4 and 5:** Ch3, work in FPdc and inc 3 sts evenly spaced, join with sl st in first dc (18 sts at the end of rnd 5).

Fasten off. Weave in end.

## Finishing

Using invisible thread, sew paper to cutecake top, stuffing the paper if it seems like it needs it.

With invisible thread and beading needle sew approx 40 seed beads sprinkled on top of icing. Try to nestle the beads into the valleys in between the rnds. (See instructions on page 11.)

This project was made with 1 skein each of

**Color A: Caron's Simply Soft** (100% acrylic, 3oz/85g, 165yd/151m), in #2614, Soft Pink

**Color B: Bernat's Satin** (100% acrylic, 3.5oz/100g, 166yd/152m), in #040130, Mocha

**Color C: Caron's Simply Soft Brites** (100% acrylic, 3oz/85g, 165yd/151m), in #9607, Limelight

# Cheeseburger with the Works

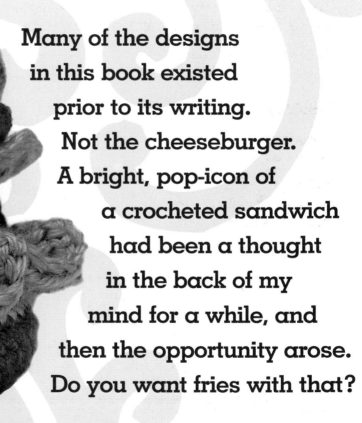

Many of the designs in this book existed prior to its writing. Not the cheeseburger. A bright, pop-icon of a crocheted sandwich had been a thought in the back of my mind for a while, and then the opportunity arose. Do you want fries with that?

## Skill Level
Intermediate

## Finished Measurements
Bun: 3"/7.6cm diameter
Lettuce: 4"/10.2cm diameter
Onions: 2½"/6.4cm diameter
Tomatoes: 2"/5.1cm diameter
Hamburger patty: 3"/7.6cm diameter

## You Will Need
Worsted weight "soft-type"
   acrylic yarn:
   Color A: brown
   Color B: copper
   Color C: green
   Color D: pale gold
   Color E: pale orange
   Color F: orchid
   Color G: red
   Color H: red-violet
*See page 2 for tips on estimating
   yarn amounts.*
Crochet hooks:
   3.5mm/E-4 *or size to obtain gauge*
   3.25mm/D-3
Tapestry needle
Invisible thread
Sewing needle

## Gauge
5 rnd gauge circle = 2"/5cm
*See page 14 for instructions on mak-
   ing a gauge circle.*

## Stitches and Techniques Used
Make ring (mr), page 4
Chain (ch)
Ch sp (chain space)
Single crochet (sc)
Invisible decrease (invdec),
   page 5
Slip stitch (sl st)
Half double crochet (hdc)
Skip (sk)
Treble crochet (tr)
Changing colors, page 11

## Instructions

### Patty (make 1)

*Note:* Patty is worked in a continuous spiral. Do not join rnds. You may wish to use a marker to indicate the beginning of the rnd.

Starting at bottom, with 3.5mm/E-4 hook and color A, mr.

**Rnd 1:** Ch 1, 6 sc in ring (6 sc).

**Rnd 2:** 2 sc in each sc (12 sc).

**Rnds 3–8:** Inc 6 sc evenly spaced (48 sc at the end of rnd 8).

**Rnd 9:** Sc in each st.

**Rnd 10:** (Invdec, sc in the next 6 sts) 6 times (42 sts).

**Rnd 11:** Sc in the next 2 sts, (invdec, sc in the next 5 sts) 5 times, invdec over the next 2 st, sc in the next 3 sts (36 sts).

**Rnd 12:** (Sc in the next 4 sts, invdec) 6 times (30 sts).

**Rnd 13:** Sc in the next 2 sts, (invdec, sc in the next 3 sts) 5 times, invdec over the next 2 sts, sc in the next st (24 sts).

**Rnd 14:** (Invdec, sc in the next 2 sts) 6 times (18 sts).

**Rnd 15:** (Sc in the next st, invdec) 6 times (12 sts).

**Rnd 16:** (Invdec, sc in the next 2 sts) 3 times (9 sts).

Fasten off, leaving an 18"/45.7cm tail. Thread tail onto tapestry needle. Close hole as illustrated on page 8. Weave in end. Flatten patty so it will fit in bun.

**Cheese (make 1)**

*Note:* Cheese is worked in joined, turned rounds. Ch 1 at beginning of rnds counts as a stitch. This technique may seem difficult at first as it is a bit of a change, but with practice you will adapt to it easily.

Starting in center, with 3.5mm/E-4 hook and color E, mr.

**Rnd 1 (right side):** Ch 1, work 5 sc in ring; join with sl st in first sc; pull starting ring closed (6 sc).

**Rnd 2 (wrong side):** Ch 1, turn, sc in first st, 2 sc in next 5 sts; join with sl st in first sc (12 sc).

**Rnd 3:** Ch 1, turn, sc in next sc, *(sc, hdc, sc) in next sc, sc in next 2 sc; rep from * 2 more times, (sc, hdc, sc) in last sc; sc in last; join with sl st in first sc (20 sts).

**Rnd 4:** Ch 1, turn, sc in next 2 sts, *(sc, hdc, sc) in next st, sc in next 4 sts; rep from * 2 more times, (sc, hdc, sc) in next st, sc in last st; join with sl st in first sc (28 sts).

**Rnd 5:** Ch 1, turn, sc in next 3 sts, *(sc, hdc, sc) in next st, sc in next 6 sts; rep from * 2 more times, (sc, hdc, sc) in next st, sc in last 2 sts; join with sl st in first sc (36 sts).

**Rnd 6:** Ch 1, turn, sc in next 4 sts, *(sc, hdc, sc) in next st, sc in next 8 sts; rep from * 2 more times, (sc, hdc, sc) in next st, sc in last 3 sts; join with sl st in first sc 44 sts).

**Rnd 7:** Ch 1, turn, sc in next 5 sts, *(sc, hdc, sc) in next st, sc in next 10 sts; rep from * 2 more times, (sc, hdc, sc) in next st, sc in last 4 sts; join with sl st in first sc (52 sts).

**Rnd 8:** Ch 1, turn, sc in next 6 sts, *(sc, hdc, sc) in next st, sc in next 12 sts; rep from * 2 more times, (sc, hdc, sc) in next st, sc in last 5 sts; do not sl st to join (60 sts).

Fasten off, leaving an 18"/45.7cm tail. Join as illustrated on page 8. Weave in ends.

### Lettuce (make 1)

*Note:* Lettuce is worked in a continuous spiral. Do not join rnds. You may wish to use a marker to indicate the beginning of the rnd.

Starting in center, with 3.5mm/E-4 hook and color C, mr.

**Rnd 1:** Ch 1, work 6 sc in ring, pull starting ring closed (6 sc).

**Rnd 2:** 2 sc in each st (12 sc).

**Rnds 3–6:** Inc 6 sc evenly spaced (36 sc at the end of rnd 6).

**Rnd 8:** Ch 8 (counts as 1 tr plus ch 3), (sk 2 st, tr in the next st, ch 3) 11 times, sk 2 sts, sl st to ch 3 of beginning ch to join (12 ch sp).

**Rnd 9:** Ch 4, 7 tr around the ch 3 post at the beginning of rnd 8, sc in the next ch sp, (8 tr around the post of the next tr from rnd 8, sc in the next ch sp) 11 times.

Fasten off, leaving an 18"/45.7cm tail. Join to first ch at beginning of rnd 9 as illustrated on page 8. Weave in ends.

### Tomato (make 2)

Note: Tomato is worked in joined rounds. Ch 1 at beginning of rnds counts as a stitch.

Starting at center, with 3.5mm/E-4 hook and color G, mr.

**Rnd 1:** Ch 1, 7 sc in ring, sl st to first sc to join (8 sc).

**Rnd 2:** Ch 1, sc in the same sp, 2 sc in the next 7 sc, sl st to first sc to join (16 sc).

**Rnd 3:** Ch 4 (counts as 1 hdc plus ch 2), sk the sp you slst-ed in to and the next st, hdc in the next st, (ch 2, sk the next st, hdc in the next st) 6 times, ch 2, sk the

last st, sl st into 2nd ch at beginning of rnd (8 ch sp).

**Rnd 4:** Ch 1, 3 sc in the next ch sp, (sk the next hdc, 4 sc in the next ch sp) 7 times (32 sts). Fasten off, leaving an 18"/45.7cm tail. Join to first sc of rnd 4 as illustrated on page 8. Weave in ends.

### Red Onion Slice (make 2)

*Note:* Onion slices are worked in joined rnds. Ch 1 at beginning of rnds counts as a stitch.

**Rnd 1:** With 3.5mm/E-4 hook and color F, ch 29. Sl st to first ch to form a ring being careful not to twist (30 sts, sl st counts as a st).

**Rnd 2:** Ch 1, sc in the same sp, sc in the next 4 sts, (2 sc in the next st, sc in the next 4 st) 5 times (36 sc).

**Rnd 3:** Change to color H. Inc 6 sc evenly spaced (42 sc).

Fasten off, leaving an 18"/45.7cm tail. Join to first sc of rnd 3 as illustrated on page 8. Weave in ends.

## Top Half of Bun (make 1)

*Note:* Bun is worked in a continuous spiral. Do not join rnds. You may wish to use a marker to indicate the beginning of the rnd.

Starting at bottom, with 3.5mm/E-4 hook and color B, mr.

**Rnd 1:** Ch 1, 6 sc in ring (6 sc).

**Rnd 2:** Ch 1, 2 sc in each st (12 sc).

**Rnd 3-6:** Inc 6 sc evenly spaced (36 sc at the end of rnd 6).

**Rnd 7-12:** Inc 3 sc evenly spaced (54 sc at the end of rnd 13).

**Rnd 11:** Switch to color E. Sc in each st.

Switch to 3.25mm/D-3 hook.

**Rnd 12:** (Sc in the next 7 st, invdec) 6 times (48 sts).

**Rnd 13:** Sc in the next 2 sts, (invdec, sc in the next 6 sts) 5 times, invdec, sc in the next 4 sts (42 sts).

**Rnd 14:** (Sc in the next 5 sts, invdec) 6 times (36 sts).

**Rnd 15:** Sc in the next 2 sts, (invdec, sc in the next 4 sts) 5 times, invdec, sc in the next 2 sts (30 sts).

**Rnd 16:** (Sc in the next 3 sts, invdec) 6 times (24 sts).

**Rnd 17:** (Invdec, sc in the next 2 sts) 6 times (18 sts).

**Rnd 18:** (Sc in the next st, invdec) 6 times (12 sts).

**Rnd 19:** (Invdec, sc in the next 2 sts) 3 times (9 sts).

Fasten off, leaving an 18"/45.7cm tail. Stuff top half of bun lightly. Close hole as illustrated on page 8. Weave in end.

## Bottom Half of Bun (make 1)

*Note:* Bun is worked in a continuous spiral. Do not join rnds. You may wish to use a marker to indicate the beginning of the rnd.

Starting at bottom, with 3.5mm/E-4 hook and color B, mr.

**Rnd 1:** Ch 1, 6 sc in ring (6 sc).

**Rnd 2:** Ch 1, 2 sc in each st (12 sc).

**Rnds 3–8:** Inc 6 sc evenly spaced (48 sc at the end of rnd 8).

**Rnds 9 and 10:** Inc 3 sc evenly spaced (54 sc at the end of rnd 9).

**Rnd 11:** Switch to color E. Sc in each sc.

Switch to 3.25mm/D-3 hook.

**Rnd 12:** (Sc in the next 7 st, invdec) 6 times (48 sts).

**Rnd 13:** Sc in the next 2 sts, (invdec, sc in the next 6 sts) 5 times, invdec, sc in the next 4 sts (42 sts).

**Rnd 14:** (Sc in the next 5 sts, invdec) 6 times (36 sts).

**Rnd 15:** Sc in the next 2 sts, (invdec, sc in the next 4 sts) 5 times, invdec, sc in the next 2 sts (30 sts).

**Rnd 16:** (Sc in the next 3 st, invdec) 6 times (24 sts).

**Rnd 17:** (Invdec, sc in the next 2 st) 6 times (18 sts).

**Rnd 18:** (Sc in the next st, invdec) 6 times (12 sts).

**Rnd 19:** (Invdec, sc in the next 2 st) 3 times (9 sts).

Fasten off, leaving an 18"/45.7cm tail. Stuff bottom half of bun lightly. Close hole as illustrated on page 8. Weave in end.

This project was made with 1 skein each of

**Color A:** Bernat's Satin (100% acrylic, 3.5oz/100g, 166yd/152m), in #040130, Mocha

**Color B:** Caron's Simply Soft (100% acrylic, 3.5oz/100g, 166yd/152m), in #2714, Copper Kettle

**Color C:** Bernat's Satin (100% acrylic, 3.5oz/100g, 166yd/152m), in #04712, Palm

**Color D:** Caron's Simply Soft (100% acrylic, 3.5oz/100g, 166yd/152m), in #2713, Buttercup

**Color E:** Caron's Simply Soft Brites (100% acrylic, 3.5oz/100g, 166yd/152m), in #2605, Mango

**Color F:** Bernat's Satin (100% acrylic, 3.5oz/100g, 166yd/152m), in #04420, Sea Shell

**Color G:** Red Heart's Soft (100% acrylic, 5 oz/140g, 256 yd/234m), in #5142, Cherry Red

**Color H:** Bernat's Satin (100% acrylic, 3.5oz/100g, 166yd/152m), in #04732, Maitai

# Mighty L'il Mouse

Something about this tiny mouse captures people's hearts. I recently made one for a preteen boy who requested one for his birthday. Imagine that! Clearly, anything is possible.

## Skill Level
Easy

## Finished Measurements
Approx 3"/7.6cm long

## You Will Need
Worsted weight "soft-type" acrylic yarn in light aqua

*See page 2 for tips on estimating yarn amounts.*

Crochet hooks:
- 3.5mm/E-4 or size to obtain gauge
- 3.25mm/D-3
- 2.75mm/C-2

Locking stitch marker

Invisible thread

Beading needle

2 black seed beads, size 6

Perle cotton, size 5, hot pink

Embroidery needle

Blush and cotton swabs

Tapestry needle

Polyester fiberfill

Knee-high nylon (optional)

PVC pellets (optional)

**Caution:** The PVC pellets listed above are not child-safe. If you're making this project for a child, use polyester fiberfill for stuffing.

## Gauge
5 rnd gauge circle = 2"/5cm

*See page 14 for instructions on making a gauge circle.*

## Stitches and Techniques Used
Make ring (mr), page 4

Double crochet (dc)

Slip stitch (sl st)

Single crochet (sc)

Half double crochet (hdc)

Invisible decrease (invdec), page 5

## Instructions

### Ears (make 2)

With 2.75mm/C-2 hook, mr.

**Rnd 1:** Ch 3, 6 dc in first ch, ch 2, sl st in ring, pull starting ring closed (7 sc).

Fasten off, leaving an 18"/45.7cm tail.

### Mouse Body

*Note:* Mouse body is worked in a continuous spiral. Do not join rnds. You may wish to use a marker to indicate the beginning of the rnd.

Starting at tip of nose, with 3.25/D-3 hook, mr.

**Rnd 1:** Ch 1, 4 sc in ring, pull starting ring closed (4 sc).

**Rnd 2:** Inc 2 sc (6 sc).

**Rnd 3:** Inc 3 sc (9 sc).

Switch to 3.5mm/E-4 hook.

**Rnd 4:** Sc in each sc.

**Rnd 5:** (2 sc in next st, 1 sc in next st) 3 times, sc in next 3 sc (12 sc).

**Rnd 6:** (2 sc in next st, 1 sc in next 2 sts) 3 times, sc in next 3 sc (15 sc).

**Rnd 7:** (2 sc in next st, 1 sc in next 3 sts) 3 times, sc in next 3 sc (18 sc).

**Rnd 8:** (2 sc in next st, 1 sc in next 4 sts) 3 times, sc in next 3 sc (21 sc).

**Rnd 9:** (2 sc in next st, 1 sc in next 5 sts) 3 times, sc in next 3 sc (24 sc).

**Rnd 10:** (2 sc in next st, 1 sc in next 6 sts) 3 times, sc in next 3 sc (27 sc).

**Rnd 11:** (2 sc in next st, 1 sc in next 7 sts) 3 times, sc in next 3 sc (30 sc).

**Rnds 12–14:** (Sc in next 3 sts, hdc in next 12 sts, sc in next 15 sts) 3 times.

**Rnd 15:** Sc in next 3 st, hdc in next 12 st, mark as end of rnd (30 sts).

**Rnd 16:** Sc in each sc.

Before you proceed to rnd 17, put your working loop on a locking marker to save it for later so you can embroider the nose and otherwise embellish the small cone shape you've crocheted to make it look like a mouse. (You could also save this work for the end, but it is much easier to hide the end of your yarn and thread this way).

Referring to photo of mouse as a guide, embellish face as follows.

•**Eyes:** Using invisible thread and beading needle, sew seed beads betweens rnds 3 and 4, four posts apart on the side of the body with the hdc.

•**Nose:** Cut a 12"/30.5cm length of Perle cotton and use the embroidery needle to sew an X in the appropriate spot.

•**Ears:** Using fastened-off ends, whipstitch ears centered below eyes between rnds 5 and 6. Dab a bit of blush in the ears using the cotton swabs.

Replace working loop on hook and proceed to rnd 17.

**Rnds 17–19:** Invdec 6 sc evenly spaced (12 sts at end of rnd 19).

Stuff mouse, using polyester fiberfill or a combination of fiberfill and half of a knee-high nylon filled with PVC pellets if desired.

Fasten off, leaving an 18"/45.7cm tail. Close hole as illustrated on page 8. Weave in end.

## Tail (make 1)

With 3.25/D-3 hook, ch 36.

**Row 1:** With 2.75mm/C-2 hook, sl st in 2nd ch and in each ch until 2nd to last ch, ch 1 (35 sts).

Fasten off, leaving an 18"/45.7cm tail. Using photo as a guide, sew on tail.

This project was made with 1 skein of
**Caron's Simply Soft in (100% acrylic, 3.5oz/100g, 166yd/152 m),
in #2705, Soft Green**

# Werner the Wiener Dog

This amigurumi was inspired by a very cute illustration of a dachshund on a notebook I wrote my patterns in. I've always thought that it pays to surround yourself with images that you find appealing.

## Skill Level
Intermediate

## Finished Measurements
Approx 4"/10.2cm tall by 14"/35.6cm long

## Materials
Worsted weight "soft-type" acrylic yarn:
  Color A: black
  Color B: coral
  Color C: light blue
  Color D: copper
See page 2 for tips on estimating yarn amounts.
Crochet hook:
  3.5mm/E-4 or size to obtain gauge
Polyester fiberfill
PVC pellets (optional)
Locking stitch marker
2 brown eyes, 15mm
Tapestry needle
Wool or wool-blend felt, red
Perle cotton, size 5, gold
Embroidery needle
Craft glue
11 silver seed beads, size 6
Small snap (for collar)
Template, page 63

**Caution:** The PVC pellets listed above are not child-safe. If you're making this project for a child, use polyester fiberfill for stuffing.

## Gauge
5 rnd gauge circle = 2"/5cm
*See page 14 for instructions on making a gauge circle.*

## Stitches and Techniques Used
Make ring (mr), page 4
Single crochet (sc)
Invisible decrease (invdec), page 5
Changing colors, page 11
Half double crochet (hdc)
Back loop only (BLO)
Blanket stitch, page 12

## Instructions

### Head

*Note:* Head is worked in a continuous spiral. Do not join rnds. You may wish to use a marker to indicate the beginning of the rnd.

Starting at tip of nose, with 3.25mm/D-3 hook and color B, mr.

**Rnd 1:** Ch 1, 6 sc in first ch, pull starting ring closed (6 sc).

**Rnd 2:** 2 sc in each sc (12 sc).

**Rnd 3:** Inc 6 evenly (18 sc).

**Rnd 4:** Sc in each sc.

**Rnd 5:** Invdec 6 (12 sc).

Switch to color A before finishing last stitch, cut color B, and work over end. Stuff nose firmly after this rnd and while working rnd 6.

**Rnd 6:** Invdec 6 times (6 sc).

The tip of the nose should be a tight ball. Switch to 3.5mm/E-4 hook.

**Rnds 7 and 8:** Inc 3 evenly spaced (12 sc at end of rnd 8).

*Note:* Make sure to stuff the rest of nose as you go along.

**Rnd 9:** (Sc in next 3 sts, 2 sc in the next st) twice, hdc in the next 3 sts, 2 hdc in the next st (15 sts).

**Rnd 10:** Sc in the next 10 sts, hdc in the next 5 sts.

**Rnd 11:** (Sc in the next 4 sts, 2sc in the next st) twice, hdc in the next 4 sts, 2hdc in the next st (18 sts).

**Rnd 12:** Sc in the next 12 sts, hdc in the next 6 sts.

**Rnd 13:** (Sc in the next 5 sts, 2sc in the next st) twice, hdc in the next 5 sts, 2hdc in the next st (21 sts).

**Rnd 14:** (Sc in the next 6 sts, 2 sc in the next st) twice, hdc in the next 6 sts, 2 hdc in the next st (24 sts).

**Rnd 15:** (Sc in the next 3 sts, 2sc in the next st) 4 times, (hdc in the next 3 sts, 2hdc in the next st) twice (30 sts).

**Rnd 16:** (Sc in the next 4 sts, 2sc in the next st) 4 times, (hdc in the next 4 sts, 2hdc in the next st) twice (36 sts).

**Rnd 17:** Sc in the next 27 sts, hdc in the next 9 sts.

**Rnd 18:** Hdc in the next 3 st, sc in the next 27 st, hdc in the next 6 sts.

**Rnd 19:** Working in sc for the rest of the head, inc 3 sc evenly spaced (39 sc).

**Rnd 20:** Inc 3 sc evenly spaced (42 sc).

**Rnd 21:** Sc in each sc.

Stop here a second to put the eyes in. Put your working loop on a locking stitch marker to save it for later. The eyes go in the valley between rnds 17 and 18—three valleys in from the edge. Make sure the nose is stuffed firmly and curves up the happy way. Orient the nose so it's smack in the middle and the head kind of looks up at you. Play with the placement of the eyes until you're happy with the spacing. The farther apart the eyes, the more innocent the dog looks; the closer together, the more predatory—until they get so close that he looks cross-eyed. To place them as I've done in this piece, put the eyes 17 posts apart, which is very far apart and looks innocent and quite sad.

Replace working loop on hook and proceed to rnd 22.

**Rnd 22:** Invdec 6 evenly spaced (36 sc).

**Rnds 23–26:** Rep rnd 22 (12 sc at end of rnd 26).

**Rnd 27:** Invdec 3 evenly spaced (9 sc).

Finish stuffing head firmly.

Fasten off, leaving an 18"/45.7cm tail. Thread tail onto tapestry needle. Close hole as illustrated on page 8. Weave in end.

## Body

*Note:* Body is worked in a continuous spiral. Do not join rnds. You may wish to use a marker to indicate the beginning of the rnd.

Starting at neck with 3.5mm/E-4 hook and color A, mr.

**Rnd 1:** Ch 1, 6 sc in ring, pull starting ring closed (6 sc).

**Rnd 2:** 2 sc in each sc (12 sc).

**Rnd 3:** Inc 6 evenly (18 sc).

**Rnd 4:** Working through BLO, sc in each sc.

**Rnd 5:** Working into both loops, sc in next 3 sc, sl st in next 6 sc, sc in next 3 sc, hdc in next 6 sc.

**Rnd 6:** (Sc in next 2 st, 2sc in next st) 6 times (24 sc).

**Rnd 7:** Sc in next 4 sc, sl st in next 8 sc, sc in next 4 sc, hdc in next 8 sc.

**Rnd 8:** (Sc in next 3 st, 2 sc in next st) 6 times (30 sc).

**Rnd 9:** Hdc in next 2 sc, sc in next 5 sc, sl st in next 10 sc, sc in next 5 sc, hdc in next 8 sc.

*Note:* When you come to the sl sts in the next rnd, work over them into the row below. This technique creates three-dimensional sculpting. Use this technique whenever sl sts are worked within the rnd for the remainder of this pattern.

**Rnd 10:** (Sc in next 4 st, 2 sc in next st) 6 times (36 sc).

**Rnd 11:** Hdc in next 4 sc, sc in next 6 sc, slst in next 12 sc, sc in next 6 st, hdc in next 8 sc.

**Rnds 12–47:** Sc in each sc.

**Rnd 48-51:** Invdec 6 sc evenly spaced (12 sc at end of rnd 51).

**Rnd 52:** Invdec 3 evenly spaced (9 sc).

Stuff body firmly.

Fasten off, leaving an 18"/45.7cm tail. Thread tail onto tapestry needle. Close hole as illustrated on page 8. Weave in end.

### Right Legs (make 2)

*Note: Legs are worked in a continuous spiral.*

Do not join rnds. You may wish to use a marker to indicate the beginning of the rnd.

Starting at bottom with 3.5mm/E-4 hook and color D, mr.

**Rnd 1:** Ch 1, 6 sc in ring, pull starting ring closed (6 sc).

**Rnd 2:** 2 sc in next st, (sc, hdc) in next st, 2 hdc in next st, (hdc, sc) in next st, 2 sc in next 2 sts (12 sts).

**Rnd 3:** 2 sc in next st, sc in next 2 sts, hdc next st, 3 hdc in next st, hdc in next st, 3 hdc in next st, hdc in next st, sc in next 2 sts, 2 sc in next 2 sts, sc in next st (18 sts).

**Rnd 4:** Sc in each st (18 sc).

**Rnd 5:** Sc in next 5 sc, invdec, sc in next 3 sc, invdec, sc in next 6 sc (16 sts).

**Rnd 6:** Sc in next 4 sts, invdec, sc in next 3 st, invdec, sc in next 5 sc (14 sts).

Change to color A.

**Rnd 7:** Sl st in next 8 sts, hdc in next 6 sts.

**Rnds 8 and 9:** Sc in next 8 sts, hdc in next 6 sts.

**Rnd 10 (short rnd):** Sc in next 2 sc. Do not finish rnd.

Stuff legs, preferably using PVC pellets as this will help the doggie to stand better. If you don't want to use the pellets for safety reasons, just stuff the legs a little extra firmly. Pinch each leg shut and make 6 sc across the top working through both thicknesses, making sure that the stuffing remains inside.

Fasten off, leaving an 18"/45.7cm tail. You will use this tail to whipstitch the legs onto the body later.

## Left Legs (make 2)

*Note:* Legs are worked in a continuous spiral. Do not join rnds. You may wish to use a marker to indicate the beginning of the rnd.

Starting at bottom with 3.5mm/E-4 hook and color D, mr.

Work rnds 1–6 of Right Legs.

**Rnd 7:** Hdc in next 6 st, sl st in next 8 sts.

**Rnds 8 and 9:** Hdc in next 6 st, sc in next 8 sts.

**Rnd 10 (short Rnd):** Sc in next 2 sc.

Follow stuffing and fastening off instructions for Right Legs.

## Ears (make 2)

*Note:* Ears are worked in a continuous spiral. Do not join rnds. You may wish to use a marker to indicate the beginning of the rnd.

Starting at bottom, with 3.5mm/E-4 hook and color D, mr.

**Rnd 1:** Ch 1, 6 sc in ring, pull starting ring closed (6 sc).

**Rnd 2:** 2 sc in each st (12 sc).

**Rnds 3–7:** Inc 6 sc evenly spaced (42 sc at the end of rnd 6).

**Rnd 8:** Invdec over next 2 sts, sc in next 17 sts, (invdec over next 2 sts) twice, sc in next 17 sts, invdec over next 2 sts (38 sts)

Fasten off, leaving an 24"/61cm tail. Fold ear in half with the decreases at the folds and use the yarn tail to whipstitch the ear closed. Do not weave in end; save it for whipstitching ear to head.

## Tail (make 1)

The tail is made at a very tight gauge. Be sure to stuff as you go. You will never get the stuffing in afterward.

*Note:* Tail is worked in a continuous spiral. Do not join rnds. You may wish to use a marker to indicate the beginning of the rnd.

Starting at tip of tail, with 2.75mm/C-2 hook and color D, mr.

**Rnd 1:** 4 sc in ring, pull starting ring closed (4 sc).

**Rnd 2:** Inc 2 sc evenly spaced (6 sc).

**Rnd 3:** Inc 1 sc (7 sc).

**Rnd 4:** Sc in each sc.

**Rnds 5–10:** Rep last 2 rnds 3 times (10 sc at end of rnd 10).

**Rnds 11–28:** Sc in each sc.

Make certain that tail is stuffed very firmly. I stuff these so firmly that they are posable without the use of any armature.

Fasten off, leaving an 18"/45.7cm tail. You will use the yarn tail to whipstitch the dog's tail on to the body later.

## Assembly

Using photo as a guide, whipstitch ears to head. The seam that you sewed shut when you folded the ear in half faces out.

Cut a 12"/30.5cm length of color D and whipstitch the head to the neck using the photo as a guide. The free front loop on rnd 4 of the body is very useful for sewing into and making sure that the head goes on straight.

Using the photo as a guide, pin the legs to the body, making sure that the dog is balanced. Whipstitch the legs to the body.

*Tip:* the legs should be very far apart from each other, almost at the rounded ends of the body.

Using the photo as a guide, pin the tail to the body, making sure it is centered. Whipstitch the tail to the body.

## Heart Appliqué

Cut a heart from the felt, using the template on page 63 as a guide.

Work blanket stitch around the edge in Perle cotton using embroidery needle.

Glue the heart to the wiener dog's bum using straight pins to keep it in place while it dries.

## Collar (make 1)

String the seed beads onto color C (see page 11) before you begin to crochet.

With 2.75mm/C-2 hook and color C, ch 25.

**Row 1:** Sc 2nd ch from hook and every ch until end, pulling up a bead in the 3rd sc and in every other sc thereafter until you run out of beads.

*Note:* A tip from the perfectionist: The collar will look nicer and much more even if you work into the bump of the starting ch instead of the more conventional method of splitting the V.

Fasten off. Weave in ends. Sew on small snap so that the collar fits tightly around neck.

This project was made with 1 skein each of

**Color A:** Caron's Simply Soft (100% acrylic, 3.5oz/100g, 166yd/152m), in #2680, Black

**Color B:** Simply Soft Brites (100% acrylic, 3.5oz/100g, 166yd/152m), in #2603, Papaya

**Color C:** Bernat's Satin (100% acrylic, 3.5oz/100g, 166yd/152m), in #04742, Lagoon

**Color D:** Caron's Simply Soft (100% acrylic, 3.5oz/100g, 166yd/152m), in #2714, Copper Kettle

# Piglet

This little piggy... started life as a sort of uninspiring prairie-dog type thing; I don't know what I was thinking. But it had potential, so I reworked the pattern into this much improved piglet. Why the spots? I can't stand to use just one color on a design.

## Skill Level

Intermediate

## Finished Measurements

Approx 5½"/14cm tall by
  5"/12.7cm wide

## You Will Need

Worsted weight "soft-type"
  acrylic yarn:
  Color A: apricot
  Color B: coral
  Color C: aqua
  Color D: copper
Perle cotton, size 5
  Color E: cream
*See page 2 for tips on estimating
  yarn amounts.*
Crochet hooks:
  3.5mm/E-4 or size to obtain gauge
  3.25mm/D-3
  2.75mm/C-2
  1.4mm/9 steel hook
Tapestry needle
Locking stitch marker
2 blue eyes, 15mm
Invisible thread
Sewing needle
Perle cotton, size 5, dark brown
Embroidery needle
Polyester fiberfill
Wool or wool-blend felt, pink
Craft glue
Straight pins
Blush and cotton swabs
Templates, page 63

## Gauge

5 rnd gauge circle = 2"/5cm
*See page 14 for instructions on
  making a gauge circle.*

## Stitches and Techniques Used

Make ring (mr), page 4
Chain (ch)
Half double crochet (hdc)
Slip stitch (sl st)
Single crochet (sc)
Double crochet (dc)
Back loop only (BLO)
Invisible decrease (invdec), page 5
French knots, page 12
Stem stitch, page 12
Repeat (rep)
Skip (sk)

## Instructions

### Round Eye Patches (make 2)

*Note:* Eye Patches are worked in joined rnds. Starting ch at beginning of rnds counts as a stitch.

Starting at center, with 1.4mm/9 steel hook and color E, mr.

**Rnd 1:** Ch 2, 13 hdc in ring, sl st to join (14 sts).

Do not pull the starting ring closed. Leave it large enough to put the shaft of the eye into later.

**Rnd2:** Ch 2, hdc in same sp, hdc in next st, sc in next 3 sts, hdc in next st, 2 hdc in next st, 2 dc in next 7 st, do not sl st to join (23 sts).

Fasten off leaving a 12"/30.5cm tail. Thread tail onto small tapestry or embroidery needle. Make invisible join (see page 8). Weave in end.

### Body and Head (make 1)

Starting at snout, with 3.5mm/E-4 hook and color A, mr.

**Rnd 1:** Ch 1, 6 sc in ring, pull starting ring closed (6 sc).

**Rnd 2:** Ch 1, 2 sc in each st (12 sc).

**Rnd 3:** Inc 6 sc evenly spaced (18 sc).

**Rnd 4:** Work over BLO.

**Rnd 5:** Sc in the next 6 st, (invdec) 3 times, sc in the next 6 sts (15 sts).

**Rnd 6:** Sc in the next 6 sts, 2 sc in the next 3 sts, sc in the next 6 sts (18 sc).

**Rnd 7:** Inc 6 sc evenly spaced (24 sc).

**Rnds 8–13:** Inc 3 sc evenly spaced (42 sc at the end of rnd 13).

**Rnd 14 and 15:** Sc in each sc.

**Rnd 16:** Sc in the next 14 sts, invdec, sc in the next 6 sts, invdec, sc in the next 7 sts, invdec, sc in the next 9 sts (39 sts).

**Rnd 17:** Sc in each st.

**Rnd 18:** Sc in the next 14 sts, invdec, sc in the next 5 sts, invdec, sc in the next 5 sts, invdec, sc in the next 9 sts (36 sts).

Take a break here a minute to make the pig's face. Put your working loop on a locking stitch marker to save it for later. Put the eye patches on the shafts of the eyes. You can tighten up the starting ring on the patches at this point if they seem really loose. Put the eyes with the eye patches now on the shafts in the valley between rnds 12 and 13, eighteen posts apart. Make sure to center the up-turn of the nose between the eyes. Take note that in the photo the wider part of the eye patch is downward, giving the piggy a questioning, almost teary-eyed look. Sew the eye patch in place using invisible thread and sewing needle. Use dark brown Perle cotton to make two French knots for nostrils. Use stem stitch for mouth.

Replace working loop on hook and proceed to rnd 19.

**Rnd 19:** Sc in each sc.

**Rnd 20:** Invdec 6 evenly (30 sts).

**Rnd 21:** Inc 3 sc evenly spaced (33 sc).

**Rnd 22:** Sc in each sc.

**Rnds 23–30:** Rep last 2 rnds 4 times (45 sc at the end of rnd 30).

**Rnds 31–33:** Inc 3 sc evenly spaced (54 sts at the end of rnd 33).

**Rnd 34 and 35:** Sc in each sc.

**Rnd 36–42:** Invdec 6 spaced evenly (12 sts at the end of rnd 42).

Stuff body.

Fasten off, leaving an 18"/45.7cm tail. Close hole as illustrated on page 8. Weave in end.

## Front Legs (make 2)

*Note:* Legs are worked in a continuous spiral. Do not join rnds. You may wish to use a marker to indicate the beginning of the rnd.

Starting at bottom, with 3.5mm/E-4 hook and color A, mr.

**Rnd 1:** Ch 1, 6 sc in ring, pull starting ring closed (6 sts).

**Rnd 2:** 2 sc in the first st, (sc, hdc) in next st, 2 hdc in next st, (hdc, sc) in next st, (2 sc next st) twice (12 sts).

**Rnd 3:** 2 sc in the next st, sc in the next 2 sts, hdc in the next st, 3 hdc in the next st, hdc in the next st, 3 hdc in the next st, hdc in the next st, sc in next 2 sts, 2 sc in the next st, sc in the next st (18 sts).

**Rnd 4:** Sc in each st.

**Rnd 5:** Sc in next 5 sts, invdec, sc in the next 3 sts, invdec, sc in the next 6 sts (16 sts).

**Rnd 6:** Sc in next 5 sts, invdec, sc in the next st, invdec, sc in the next 6 sts (14 sts).

**Rnd 7:** Sc in next 4 sts, invdec, sc in the next st, invdec, sc in the next 5 sts (12 sts).

**Rnds 8–11:** Sc in each sc.

**Rnd 12:** (Invdec, sc in the next 2 sts) 3 times (9 sts).

Fasten off, leaving an 18"/45.7cm tail. Stuff foot. Close hole as illustrated on page 8. Weave in end.

Cut an 18"/45.7cm length of color A for each leg. Using the photo as a guide, whipstitch legs in place.

Cut two front feet soles out of felt using the template on page 63 as a guide. Glue them to bottoms of front feet, using straight pins to keep them in place while they dry.

## Back Feet (make 2 with A)

*Note:* Back feet are worked in joined, oval-shaped rnds. Ch 1 at beginning of rnds 1–4 counts as a stitch.

Do not mr to begin and do not sl st to join rnds except as noted. At rnd 5, you begin working in spirals.

**Rnd 1:** With 3.5mm/E-4 hook and color A, ch 5, 2 sc in second ch from hook, sc in next 2 ch, 3 hdc in last ch, turn and work along the other side of the chain, working into the unused loops, sc in next 2 ch, sl st to the top of the first sc to join (join all following rnds in this manner until rnd 5) (10 sts).

**Rnd 2:** Ch 1 (at the beginning of this and every rnd until rnd 5), sc in same space, sc in next 3 sts, (sc, 2 hdc) in the next st, 2 hdc in the next st, (2 hdc, sc) in the next st, sc in next 3 sts, sl st to the top of the first sc to join (16 sts).

**Rnd 3:** Ch 1, 2 sc in same space, sc in next 4 sts, (sc, 2 hdc) in the next st, hdc in next 4 sts, (2 hdc, sc) in the next st, sc in next 3 sts, 2 sc in the next st, sl st to the top of the first sc to join (22 sts).

**Rnd 4:** Ch 1, sc in same space, sc in next 6 sts, (sc, 2 hdc) in the next st, hdc in next 6 sts, (2 hdc, sc) in the next st, sc in next 6, sl st to the top of the first sc to join (26 sts).

**Rnd 5:** Do not ch 1. Sk the sp you slst-ed into. Sc into the next st. See how your work is slanting? It should look like that. You have just switched to working a spiral. Congrats! Sc in the next 5 sts, invdec, sc in the next 7 sts, invdec, sc the 7 sts (23 sts).

Continue working in spirals for remainder of foot.

**Rnd 6:** Invdec, sc in the next 5 sts, (invdec) twice, sc in the next st, (invdec) twice, sc in the next 5 sts, invdec (17 sts).

**Rnd 7:** Invdec, sc in the next 5 sts, invdec over the next 3 sts, sc in the next 5 sts, invdec (13 sts).

Fasten off leaving an 18"/45.7cm tail. Stuff foot very lightly. Pinch hole closed so that it makes a straight seam and whipstitch it shut with the yarn tail. Weave in end. This seam is now at the bottom of the foot. Cut an 18"/45.7cm length of color A for each foot. Using photo as a guide, whipstitch feet in place using yarn and tapestry needle.

Cut two back feet soles out of felt using the template on page 63 as a guide. Glue them to bottom of back feet using straight pins to keep them in place while they dry.

## Ears (make 2)

*Note:* Ears are worked in a continuous spiral. Do not join rnds. You may wish to use a marker to indicate the beginning of the rnd.

Starting at tip, with 3.5mm/E-4 hook and color A, mr.

**Rnd 1:** Ch 1, 4 sc in ring, pull starting ring closed (4 sc).

**Rnds 2–8:** Inc 2 sc evenly spaced (18 sc at the end of rnd 8).

**Rnds 9 and 10:** Sc in each sc.

Fasten off leaving a 18"/45.7cm tail. Flatten ear and fold in half. There should be four layers of crochet. Using the yarn tail, whipstitch these layers together. Dab a bit of blush in the ears using the cotton swabs. Do not weave in end; instead, referring to photo as a guide, use it to whipstitch ears to head.

## Tail (make 1)

With 2.75mm/C-2 hook and color A, ch 9 leaving an 18"/45.7cm tail at the beginning; turn.

**Row 1:** Sk the first ch, sc in the next 2 ch, 2 sc in the next 6 chs (14 sc).

Fasten off leaving a 18"/45.7cm tail. Using both yarn tails, sew the pig's tail to its body.

## Spots

*Note:* Spots are worked in joined rnds. Chs at beginning of rnds count as a stitch.

### Large (make 1 of each out of colors B, C, and D)

Starting at center, with 2.75mm/C-2 hook, mr.

**Rnd 1:** Ch 2, 7 hdc in ring, sl st to join, pull starting ring closed (8 sts).

**Rnd 2:** Ch 2, hdc in same space, 2 hdc in each st. Do not sl st (16 sts).

Fasten off leaving a 12"/30.5cm tail. Thread yarn onto tapestry needle. Make invisible join (see page 8 for instructions). Weave in end.

### Small (make 1 of each out of colors B, C, and D)

Starting at center, with 2.75mm/C-2 hook, mr.

**Rnd 1:** Ch 1, 6 sc in ring, do not join, pull starting ring closed (7 sts).

Fasten off leaving a 12"/30.5cm tail. Thread yarn onto tapestry needle. Make invisible join (see page 8 for instructions). Weave in end.

Referring to the photo, sew the spots onto the pig's back and rump using the sewing needle and invisible thread.

This project was made with 1 skein each of

**Color A:** Caron's Simply Soft (100% acrylic, 3.5oz/100g, 166yd/152m), in #2715, Seashell

**Color B:** Caron's Simply Soft Brites (100% acrylic, 3.5oz/100g, 166yd/152m), in #2603, Papaya

**Color C:** Caron's Simply Soft Brites (100% acrylic, 3.5oz/100g, 166yd/152m), in #2608, Blue Mint

**Color D:** Caron's Simply Soft (100% acrylic, 3.5oz/100g, 166yd/152m), in #2714, Copper Kettle

**Color E:** DMC's Perle cotton, size 5, in #0002, Ecru

# Friends Forever Fawn

Straight out of a children's fairytale, this sweet fawn's eyes will melt your heart.

## Skill Level
Advanced

## Finished Measurements
Approx 8"/20.3cm tall by 7"/17.8cm long

## You Will Need
Worsted weight "soft-type" acrylic yarn:
   Color A: black
   Color B: copper
   Color C: pale gold
*See page 2 for tips on estimating yarn amounts.*
Crochet hooks:
   3.5mm/E-4 or size to obtain gauge
   2.75mm/C-2
Locking stitch marker
Wool or wool-blend felt, burgundy
Wool or wool-blend felt, pink
Perle cotton, size 5, black
Embroidery needle
2 black eyes, 15mm
Polyester fiberfill
Tapestry needle
Blush and cotton swabs
PVC pellets
Knee-high nylon (optional)
Invisible thread
Beading needle
Approx 13 flat white sequins
Approx 13 cream seed beads, size 10
Template, page 63

**Caution:** The PVC pellets listed above are not child-safe. This project is not appropriate for young children.

## Gauge
5 rnd gauge circle = 2"/5cm
*See page 14 for instructions on making a gauge circle.*

## Stitches and Techniques Used
Make ring (mr), page 4
Chain (ch)
Single crochet (sc)
Invisible decrease (invdec), page 5
Changing colors, page 11
Repeat (rep)
Back loop only (BLO)
Skip (sk)
Single crochet
   2 together (sc2tog)
Double crochet (dc)
Slip stitch (sl st)

# Instructions

## Head (make 1)

*Note:* Head is worked in a continuous spiral. Do not join rnds. You may wish to use a marker to indicate the beginning of the rnd.

Starting at front of muzzle, with color C and 3.5mm/E-4 hook, mr.

**Rnd 1:** Ch 1, 6 sc in ring, pull starting ring closed (6 sc).

**Rnd 2:** 2 sc in each st (12 sc).

**Rnds 3 and 4:** Inc 6 sc evenly spaced (24 sc at the end of rnd 4).

**Rnd 5:** Sc in next 8 sts, (invdec over next 2 sts, sc in next st) twice, invdec over next 2 st, sc in next 8 sts (21 sts).

**Rnd 6:** Sc in next 8 sts, (invdec over next 2 sts) 3 times, sc in next 7 sts (18 sts).

Switch to color B.

**Rnd 7:** Inc 6 sc evenly spaced (24 sc).

**Rnd 8:** Inc 3 sc evenly spaced (27 sc).

**Rnd 9:** Sc in each sc.

**Rnds 10–19:** Rep rnds 8 and 9 (42 st at the end of rnds 18 and 19).

**Rnds 20–24:** Invdec 6 sc evenly spaced (12 st at the end of rnd 24).

Put your working loop on a locking stitch marker to save it for later.

Cut eye patches out of felt using the template on page 63 as a guide. Glue the pink circles to the burgundy almond shapes and allow the glue to dry.

With black perle cotton, using photo as a guide, embroider eyelashes, making sure to reverse the direction of the lashes for each eye.

Put the eyes with the eye patches on the shafts in the valley between rnds 13 and 14, sixteen posts apart. Make sure to center the up-turn of the muzzle between the eyes.

Fasten off, leaving an 18"/45.7cm tail.

Stuff head, making sure to stuff all the way into muzzle.

Thread yarn tail onto tapestry needle. Close hole as illustrated on page 8. Weave in end.

## Nose (make 1)

*Note:* Nose is worked in a continuous spiral. Do not join rnds. You may wish to use a marker to indicate the beginning of the rnd.

Starting at tip, with 2.5mm/C-2 hook and color A, mr.

**Rnd 1:** Ch 1, 6 sc in ring, pull starting ring closed (6 sts).

**Rnd 2:** 2 sc in each st (12 sts).

**Rnds 3 and 4:** Work even in sc.

**Rnd 5:** Invdec 3 sc evenly spaced (9 sts).

Stuff nose firmly.

Fasten off, leaving an 18"/45.7cm tail. Thread onto tapestry needle. Close hole as illustrated on page 8. Do not weave in end. Whipstitch nose to muzzle using yarn tail.

## Ears (make 2)

Starting at tip, with 3.5mm/E-4 hook and color B, mr.

**Rnd 1:** Ch 1, 4 sc in ring, pull starting ring closed (4 sts).

**Rnds 2–8:** Inc 2 sc evenly spaced (18 st at the end of rnd 8).

**Rnds 9 and 10:** Work even in sc.

Fasten off leaving a 18"/45.7cm tail. Flatten ear and fold in half. There should be four layers of crochet. Using yarn tail, whipstitch these layers together. Do not weave in end. Dab a bit of blush in the ears using the cotton swabs.

Using photo as a guide, whipstitch ears to head.

## Body (make 1)

Starting at neck, with 3.5mm/E-4) hook and color B, mr.

**Rnd 1:** Ch 1, 6 sc in ring, pull starting ring closed (6 sc).

**Rnd 2:** 2 sc in each st (12 sc).

**Rnd 3:** Working thru BLO for entire rnd, sc in next 2 sts, sl st in next 4 sts, sc in next 2 sts, hdc in next 4 sts (12 sts).

*Note:* When you come to the sl sts in the next round, work over them into the row below. This technique creates three-dimensional sculpting. Use this technique whenever sl sts are worked within the rnd for the remainder of this pattern.

**Rnd 4:** (Sc in next 3 sts, 2 sc in next st) twice, hdc in next 3 sts, 2 hdc in next st (15 sts).

**Rnd 5:** Sc in next 3 sts, sl st in next 5 sts, sc in next 2 sts, hdc in next 5 sts (15 sts).

**Rnd 6:** (Sc in next 4 sts, 2 sc in next sts) twice, hdc in next 4 sts, 2 hdc in next st (18 sts).

**Rnd 7:** Sc in next 3 sts, sl st in next 6 sts, sc in next 3 sts, hdc in next 6 sts (18 sts).

**Rnd 8:** (Sc in next 5 sts, 2 sc in next st) twice, hdc in next 5 sts, 2 hdc in next st (21 sts).

**Rnd 9:** (Sc in next 6 sts, 2 sc in next st) twice, hdc in next 6 sts, 2 hdc in next st (24 sts).

**Rnd 10:** (Sc in next 3 sts, 2 sc in next st) 4 times, (hdc in next 3 sts, 2 hdc in next st) twice (30 sts).

**Rnd 11:** (Sc in next 4 sts, 2 sc in next st) 4 times, (hdc in next 4 sts, 2 hdc in next st) twice (36 sts).

**Rnd 12:** Sc in next 27 sts, hdc in next 9 sts.

**Rnd 13:** Hdc in next 3 sts, sc in next 27 sts, hdc in next 6 sts.

**Rnd 14:** Hdc in next 6 sts, sc in next 27 sts, hdc in next 3 sts.

**Rnd 15:** Hdc in next 9 sts, sc in next 27 sts.

**Rnds 16–21:** Sc in each sc.

**Rnds 22–25:** Invdec 6 sc evenly spaced (12 sc at the end of rnd 25).

Fasten off, leaving an 18"/45.7cm tail. Stuff the body, making especially certain that the neck is stuffed firmly. I find that it helps the fawn to balance nicely if I put half a knee-high nylon filled with PVC pellets in its belly in addition to polyester fiberfill. To do this, stuff the fawn about halfway and put an empty knee-high that has been cut in half in its belly. Open the knee-high up and put a few small handfuls of pellets in it; tie it with an overhand knot and then finish off the stuffing with some more fiberfill.

*Note:* It is essential to put PVC pellets in legs or else fawn will not stand up properly.

Thread yarn tail onto tapestry needle. Close hole as illustrated on page 8. Weave in end.

## Front Legs (make 2)

*Note:* Legs are worked in a continuous spiral. Do not join rnds. You may wish to use a marker to indicate the beginning of the rnd.

Starting at bottom, with 3.5mm/E-4 hook and color A, mr.

**Rnd 1:** Ch 1, 6 sc in ring, pull starting ring closed (6 sc).

**Rnd 2:** 2 sc in next st, (sc, hdc) in next st, 2 hdc in next st, (hdc, sc) in next st, 2 sc in next 2 sts (12 sts).

**Rnd 3:** 2 sc in next st, sc in next 2 sts, hdc next st, 3 hdc in next st, hdc in next st, 3 hdc in next st, hdc in next st, sc in next 2 sts, 2 sc in next st, sc in next st (18 sts).

**Rnd 4:** Sc in each sc.

**Rnd 5:** Sc in next 5 sts, invdec over next 2 sts, sc in next 3 sts, invdec over next 2 sts, sc in next 6 sts (16 sts).

Switch to color B.

**Rnd 6:** Sc in next 4 sts, invdec over next 2 sts, sc in next 3 sts, invdec over next 2 sts, sc in next 5 sts (14 sts).

**Rnds 7 and 8:** Sc in each sc.

**Rnd 9:** Sc in next 2 sts, invdec over next 2 sts, sc in next 10 sts (13 sts).

**Rnd 10 and 11:** Sc in each sc.

**Rnd 12:** Sc in next 9 sts, invdec over next 2 sts, sc in next 2 sts (12 sts).

**Rnd 13–20:** Sc in each sc.

**Rnd 21:** Sc in next 2 sts, 2 sc in next st, sc in next 9 sts (13 sc).

**Rnd 22:** Sc in next 12 sts, 2 sc in next st (14 sc).

**Rnd 23:** Sc in next 6 sts, 2 sc in next st, sc in next 7 sts (15 sc).

**Rnd 24:** Sc in next 2 sts, 2 sc in next st, sc in next 12 sts (16 sc).

**Rnd 25:** Sc in next 4 sts, 2 sc in next st, sc in next 11 sts (17 sc).

**Rnd 26:** Sc in next 2 sts, hdc in next st, 2 hdc in next 2 sts, hdc in next st, sc in next 11 sts (19 sts).

**Rnd 27:** Sc in next 3 sts, (invdec over next 2 sts) 3 times, sc in next 10 sts (16 sts).

Stuff each leg with PVC pellets. If you find that the PVC is popping out if the crochet, you can line the inside of the legs with half of a knee-high nylon before stuffing them to keep the pellets from coming out. Be thrifty and use the second top half of the nylon, too. Just knot the cut end with an overhand knot before using it.

*Note:* It is essential to put PVC pellets in legs or else fawn will not stand up properly.

## Close Top of Leg

The next few rows neatly close the top of the fawn's leg and give you a handy tab for sewing the leg onto the body.

**Row 1:** Sc in next 5 sts. Turn with no ch. Pinch leg shut.

**Row 2:** Sc in next 7 sts through both thicknesses. Because you did not ch, the turn will be tight. To make this easier, sk the last st of row 1. Turn with no ch.

**Row 3:** Sk first st, sc in next 4 sts, sc2tog.

Fasten off leaving a 18"/45.7cm tail. Do not weave in end. Using photo as a guide, whipstitch front legs to body.

## Hind Legs

Rep rnds 1–12 of Front Legs—12 sts.

**Rnd 13-17:** Work even in sc.

**Rnd 18:** (2 hdc in next st) twice, sc in next 4 sts, sl st in next 2 sts, sc in next 4 sts (14 sts).

**Rnds 19 and 20:** Work even in sc.

**Rnd 21:** Sc in next 4 sts, 2 sc in next st, sc in next 9 sts (15 sts).

**Rnd 22:** Sc in next 14 sts, 2 sc in next st (16 sts).

**Rnd 23:** Sc in next 9 sts, (2 sc in next st) twice, sc in next 5 sts (18 sts).

**Rnd 24:** Sc in next 9 sts, (invdec over next 2 sts) twice, sc in next 5 sts (16 sts).

**Rnds 25 and 26:** Work even in sc.

Work remainder of Hind Legs as for Front Legs, skipping rnd 27.

## Tail (make 1)

Starting at tip, with 3.5mm/E-4 hook and color B, mr.

**Rnd 1:** ch 1, 4 sc in ring, pull starting ring closed (4 sts).

**Rnds 2–6:** Inc 2 sc evenly spaced (14 sts at the end of rnd 6).

**Rnd 7:** Work even in sc.

Fasten off leaving a 18"/45.7cm tail.

If desired, cut 1yd/91.4cm of yarn in color D, unwind the strands, and use two of them to embroider straight stitches on the underside of the tail.

Flatten tail and fold in half. There should be four layers of crochet. Using yarn tail, whipstitch these layers together. Do not weave in end. Using photo as a guide, whipstitch tail to body.

Cut a 12"/30.5cm length of color B and whipstitch the head to neck using the photo as a guide. The free front loop on rnd 3 of the body is very useful for sewing into; note that unlike Werner the Weiner Dog, whose head was sewn on straight, the Fawn's head is at a slight angle.

Using photo as a guide, sew sequins and beads on to the fawn's back.

This project was made with 1 skein each of

**Color A:** Caron's Simply Soft (100% acrylic, 3.5oz/100g, 166yd/152m), in #2680, Black

**Color B:** Caron's Simply Soft (100% acrylic, 3.5oz/100g, 166yd/152m), in #2714, Copper Kettle

**Color C:** Caron's Simply Soft (100% acrylic, 3.5oz/100g, 166yd/152m), in #2713, Buttercup

# Benny the Monkey

This monkey is one of my most popular humanoid dolls. I have made this little guy in a wide variety of ways—as a girl monkey wearing a miniskirt and figure skates, as a boy monkey in pants eating chocolate cream pie, and here in everyday bumming-around shorts and flip-flops, just to name a few. In other words, have fun—there are endless creative options to explore.

## Skill Level
Intermediate

## Finished Measurements
Approx 12"/30.5cm tall

## You Will Need
Worsted weight "soft-type" acrylic yarn:
   Color A: berry blue
   Color B: lime green
   Color C: red
   Color D: pale gold
   Color E: black
*See page 2 for tips on estimating yarn amounts.*
Crochet hooks:
   3.5mm/E-4 or size to obtain gauge
   3mm/D-3
   3.75mm/F-5
   4mm/G-6
Tapestry needle
Polyester fiberfill
2 eyes of any color, 9mm (for arm joints)
2 black eyes, 12mm
Locking stitch markers
Invisible thread
Black embroidery floss
2 black seed beads, size 8 (optional)
Large-headed seaming pins
Wool or wool-blend felt, white
Perle cotton, size 5, gold
Embroidery needle
Craft glue
PVC pellets (optional)
Knee-high nylon (if using PVC pellets)

Straight pins
Template, page 63

**Caution:** The PVC pellets listed above are not child-safe. If you're making this project for a child, use polyester fiberfill for stuffing.

## Gauge
5 rnd gauge circle = 2"/5cm
*See page 14 for instructions on making a gauge circle.*

## Stitches and Techniques Used
Make ring (mr), page 4
Chain (ch)
Single crochet (sc)
Invisible Decrease (invdec), page 5
Bobble, page 5
Changing colors, page 11
Slip stitch (sl st)
Half double crochet (hdc)
Double crochet (dc)
French knot, page 12
Stem stitch, page 12
Blanket stitch, page 12

# Instructions

*Note:* Sometimes, before or after a color change, I work an uncounted rnd of sl sts as indicated in the instructions. Do not work back into the sl sts. Instead, work the next rnd into the loops at the top of the rnd below. This smoothes out the color change. Be careful to keep your stitch count correct. If you find this difficult, you can skip these rows and work chain stitch embroidery to cover the color change after you are finished crocheting the doll. It gives the same effect but leaves more ends to weave in.

## Arm (make 2)

*Note:* Arms are worked in a continuous spiral. Do not join rnds. You may wish to use a marker to indicate the beginning of the rnd.

Starting at fingertips, with 3.5mm/E-4 hook and color B, mr.

**Rnd 1:** Ch 1, work 6 sc in ring, pull starting ring closed (6 sc).

**Rnd 2:** 2 sc in each sc around (12 sc).

**Rnd 3:** *2 sc in next sc, sc in next sc; rep from * around (18 sc).

**Rnds 4 and 5:** Sc in each sc.

**Rnd 6:** Sc in next 16 sc, invdec over last 2 sc (17 sc).

**Rnd 7:** Sc in next 7 sts, invdec over next 2 sts, sc in next 7 sts, make bobble in next st (16 sts).

**Rnd 8:** Sc in next 14 sts, invdec over next 2 sts (15 sts).

**Rnd 9:** Invdec over next 2 sts, sc in next 13 sts (14 sts).

Change to color A.

**Rnd 10:** Sc in next 6 sts, invdec over next 2 sts, sc in next 6 sts (13 sts).

**Rnd 11:** Sc in next 11 sts, invdec over next 2 sts (12 sts).

**Rnd 12:** Sc in next 4 sts, invdec over next 2 sts, sc in next 6 sts (11 sts).

**Rnd 13:** Sc in next 9 sts, invdec over next 2 sts (10 sts).

**Rnds 14–28:** Sc in each sc.

Switch to color C. Work an uncounted rnd of sl st.

**Rnds 29–33:** Sc in each sc.

Fasten off, leaving an 18"/45.7cm tail. Stuff arm. To make the shoulder joint, put a 9mm eye inside each arm with the shaft poking out in the first valley down from the top, lining up with the bobble thumb. Put a bit more stuffing on top of the shoulder. Close hole as illustrated on page 8. Weave in ends. Use an 18"/45.7cm length of yarn to sew through both layers of the arm to create a dent for the elbow in the 12th valley down from the top.

## Face (make 1)

With 4.25mm/G-6 hook and color B, ch 14. Change to 3.5mm/E-4 hook.

**Rnd 1:** Working in back bumps of foundation ch, sc in second and each ch across (13 sc).

**Rnd 2:** Pivot work to work along opposite side of foundation, sk first sc, 6 dc in next sc, sk 1 sc, sc in next 7 sc, sk 1 sc, 6 dc in next sc, sk last sc; join with sl st to top of first sc in rnd 1 to join (32 st).

**Rnd 3:** Ch 2, (hdc, sc) in same st as join, sc in next 11 sc, (sc, hdc) in next sc, 2 dc in next 6 dc, hdc in next st, sk 2 sc, sl st in next sc, sk 2 sc, hdc in next st, 2 dc in next 6 dc, do not join.

Fasten off. Make an invisible join as illustrated on page 8. Weave in ends.

Put 12mm black eyes into stitches with 6 dcs in them. If the holes are not big enough, make them larger with the end of a rattail comb or something else pointy. Set face aside for later.

## Muzzle (make 1)

*Note:* Muzzle is worked in a continuous spiral. Do not join rnds. You may wish to use a marker to indicate the beginning of the rnd.

Starting at bottom, with 3.5mm/E-4 hook and color B, mr.

**Rnd 1:** Ch 1, 6 sc in ring, pull starting ring closed (6 sc).

**Rnd 2:** Inc 6 sts (12 sc).

**Rnds 3–23:** Sc in each sc.

**Rnd 9:** (Invdec, sc in next 2 st) 3 times (9 sc).

Fasten off, leaving an 18"/45.7cm tail. Close hole as illustrated on page 8. Weave in end. Set muzzle aside for later.

## Ears (make 2)

*Note:* Ears are worked in a continuous spiral. Do not join rnds. You may wish to use a marker to indicate the beginning of the rnd.

Starting at tip, with 3.5mm/E-4 hook and color A, mr.

**Rnd 1:** Ch 1, work 6 sc in ring; do not join, pull starting ring closed (6 sc).

**Rnd 2:** 2 sc in each sc around (12 sc).

**Rnd 3:** (Sc in next sc, 2 sc in next sc) 6 times (18 sc).

**Rnd 4:** (Sc in next 7 sc, invdec over next 2 sts) twice (16 sts).

**Rnd 5:** (Sc in next 6 sc, invdec over next 2 sts) twice (14 sts).

**Rnd 6:** (Sc in next 5 sc, invdec over next 2 sts) twice (12 sts).

**Rnd 7:** (Sc in next 4 sc, invdec over next 2 sts) twice (10 sts).

Fasten off, leaving an 18"/45.7cm tail for sewing ear to head. Set ear aside for later.

## Body (make 1)

*Note:* Body is worked in a continuous spiral. Do not join rnds. You may wish to use a marker to indicate the beginning of the rnd.

Starting at top of head, with 3.5mm/E-4 hook and color A, mr.

**Rnd 1:** Ch 1, work 6 sc in ring, pull starting ring closed (6 sc).

**Rnd 2:** 2 sc in each sc around (12 sc).

**Rnds 3–5:** Inc 6 sc evenly spaced around. Avoid placing increases in the same place every round (30 sc at end of rnd 5).

**Rnds 6–13:** Inc 3 sc evenly spaced around (54 sc at end of rnd 13).

**Rnds 14 and 15:** Sc in each sc.

**Rnds 16–19:** Sc around, invdec 6 times evenly spaced around. Avoid placing decreases in the same place every round (30 sts at end of rnd 19).

**Rnd 20:** (Invdec over next 2 sts) 15 times (15 sts).

Place working yarn loop on a locking stitch marker and position the yarn tail at the back of the head. You'll now assemble the head.

The face and eyes are sewn on first. If you look at the texture of the crochet you'll see that the rounds form ridges and valleys. If you look even closer at the texture you'll see tiny posts in the valleys between rounds. Place the eyes (which are now connected to the face, of course) on the posts in the third valley above the first decrease round. Another way of saying this is to put them between rounds 13 and 14, thirteen posts apart, making sure eyes are centered in the doll's face. Once you know where you want the eyes to be, use something like the end of a rattail comb to poke a large hole into the crochet. Don't worry about hurting the crochet; it should be quite strong since you used such a small hook. Poke the eyes with the patches on the shafts through to the inside of the head and fasten with the washers that came with them. You may have to stretch the face a bit to get them to fit. That's OK.

Sew muzzle onto head in between eyes using invisible thread, using photo as a guide. Make a French knot with two strands of embroidery floss, or sew on one black size-8 seed bead for each nostril. With two strands of embroidery floss, embroider a straight line for the mouth using stem stitch.

Using the yarn tails you left on the ears and a tapestry needle, sew them in place. Weave the ends into the head.

For both the ears and the muzzle, it's helpful to stuff the head first, pin these things in place using large-headed pins, and then sew them on.

Make sure the head is stuffed firmly. After the head is rounded out, tack the face down with invisible thread as well.

Replace working loop on hook and switch to color C.

Work an uncounted rnd of sl sts.

**Rnd 21:** Sc around increasing 3 sc evenly spaced around (18 sc).

**Rnd 22:** Sc in each sc.

**Rnds 23 and 24:** Rep rnds 21 and 22 (21 sc).

To attach the arms, put the eye shafts at the shoulders into body in the valley between rnds 22 and 23, eleven posts apart in the front. Put washers on eye shafts to secure arms.

**Rnds 25–34:** Rep last 2 rnds 5 times (36 sc).

**Rnds 35–37:** Sc in each sc.

Work an uncounted rnd of sl sts.

## Shorts

Switch to color D and 3.75mm/F-5 hook.

**Rnd 1:** Working through front loop only of st for entire rnd, sc in each sc around. When you get to the stitch just before the center back ch 3, sk 3 stitches. This is hole for the tail.

**Rnd 2:** Sc in each sc around, sc into the chs when you come to them (36 sc).

**Rnds 3–8:** Sc in each sc.

**Rnd 9:** Sl st in each sc.

Fasten off. Weave in ends.

Roll shorts to expose back loop of rnd 37. Pull up a loop of color A in the last stitch of rnd 37 and proceed as follows:

**Rnds 38–42:** Working into the unused loops of rnd 37 of body, sc in each sc.

Stuff the body, using polyester fiberfill or PVC pellets (if desired).

Now the body will be divided to form the legs. Place working yarn loop on a locking stitch marker or safety pin. You should have a head with a tubular body and arms attached.

Find center front point: This point lies along the lower edge of the body and lines up with the nose of your creature. Place a pin (large-headed seaming pins are particularly useful for this) or stitch marker between two stitches to mark center front point. Count 18 stitches on either side of the center point. Place a second stitch marker or pin between two stitches at the center back. The center front and back points divide the body into a left half and a right half.

## Left Leg

Put working loop back on hook.

**Rnd 1:** Sc in each sc to the center back marker, sk next 18 sts (leaving them for Right Leg), remove markers, sc in each sc to the end of the round (18 sts).

**Rnds 2–20:** Sc in each sc.

**Rnd 21:** Sc in each sc around, inc once (19 sc).

**Rnd 22:** Sc in each sc.

**Rnds 23–28:** Rep last 2 rnds 3 times (22 sc).

Mark center front stitch of leg with pin or stitch marker.

**Rnd 29:** Sc in each sc to 2 sc before marker, 3 hdc in next sc, hdc in next sc, (next sc should be marked), remove marker and hdc in next sc, hdc in next sc, 3 hdc in next sc, sc in each sc to end of rnd (26 sts).

Switch to color B.

**Rnd 30:** Sc in each st until 2nd hdc of rnd 29, 3 hdc in next st, hdc in next 5 sts, 3 hdc in next st, sc in each st to end of rnd (30 sts).

**Rnd 31:** Sc in each sc until 2nd hdc of rnd 30, 3 hdc in next st, hdc in next 7 sts, 3 hdc in next st, sc in each st to end of rnd (34 sts).

## Left Bobble Toes

**Rnd 32:** Work as follows. Note that the bobbles are made with a different number of sts to create toes that are different sizes.

Sc in each sc until 3rd hdc of rnd 31.

Make bobble in next st: (YO, insert hook in next st, YO and draw up a loop, YO and draw through 2 loops on hook) 6 times, YO and draw through all 7 loops on hook.

Sc in next st.

Make bobble in next st: (YO, insert hook in st, YO and draw up a loop, YO and draw through 2 loops on hook) 5 times, YO and draw through all 6 loops on hook.

Sc in next st.

Make bobble in next st:sc in next st, (YO, insert hook in st, YO and draw up a loop, YO and draw through 2 loops on hook) 4 times, YO and draw through all 5 loops on hook.

Sc in next st.

Make bobble in next st: (YO, insert hook in st, YO and draw up a loop, YO and draw through 2 loops on hook) 4 times, YO and draw through all 5 loops on hook.

Sc in next st.

Make bobble in next st: (YO, insert hook in st, YO and draw up a loop, YO and draw through 2 loops on hook) 3 times, YO and draw through all 4 loops on hook, sc in each st to end of rnd (34 sts).

Switch to color E.

**Rnd 33:** Sl st in each sc.

Fasten off, leaving an 18"/45.7cm tail. Weave in end. Stuff the leg with polyester fiberfill.

## Right Leg

With the 'gurumi's back facing you, sk 7 st, Join color A in next sc.

**Rnd 1:** Sc in each sc around (18 sts).

**Rnds 2–31:** Work as for rnds 2–31 of Left Leg.

## Right Bobble Toes

**Rnd 32:** Work as follows. Note that the bobbles are made with a different number of sts to create toes that are different sizes.

Sc in each sc until 3rd hdc of rnd 31.

Make bobble in next st: (YO, insert hook in st, YO and draw up a loop, YO and draw through 2 loops on hook) 3 times, YO and draw through 4 loops on hook.

Sc in next st.

Make bobble in next st: (YO, insert hook in st, YO and draw up a loop, YO and draw through 2 loops on hook) 4 times, YO and draw through 5 loops on hook.

Sc in next st.

Make bobble in next st: (YO, insert hook in st, YO

and draw up a loop, YO and draw through 2 loops on hook) 4 times, YO and draw through 5 loops on hook.

Sc in next st.

Make bobble in next st: (YO, insert hook in st, YO and draw up a loop, YO and draw through 2 loops on hook) 5 times, YO and draw through 6 loops on hook.

Sc in next st.

Make bobble in next st: (YO, insert hook in st, YO and draw up a loop, YO and draw through 2 loops on hook) 6 times, YO and draw through 7 loops on hook, sc in each st to end of rnd (34 sts).

Switch to color E.

**Rnd 33:** Sl st in each sc.

Fasten off, leaving an 18"/45.5cm tail. Weave in end. Stuff the leg, using polyester fiberfill.

## Sole of Foot (make 2)

*Note:* Soles of feet are worked in joined, oval-shaped rnds. Ch 1 at beginning of rnds counts as a stitch.

With 3mm/D-3 hook and color E, ch 7.

**Rnd 1:** Working in back bumps of foundation ch, sc in second ch from hook, sc in next 4 ch, 3 hdc in last ch; working along opposite side of beginning ch, sc in next 5 ch; join with sl st in first sc (14 sts).

**Rnd 2:** Ch 1, 2 sc in same st as join, sc in next 4 sts, 3 hdc in next st, hdc in next st, 3 hdc in next st, sc in next 4 sts, 3 sc in last st, join with sl st in first sc (21 sts).

**Rnd 3:** Ch 1, 2 sc in same st as join, sc in next 6 sts, 3 hdc in next st, hdc in next 3 sts, 3 hdc in next st, sc in next 8 sts, join with sl st in first sc (26 sts).

**Rnd 4:** Ch 1, 2 sc in same st as join, sc in next st, 2 sc in next st, sc in next 6 st, 3 hdc in next st, hdc in next 5 sts, 3 hdc in next st, sc in next 6 sts, 2 sc in next st, sc in next st, 2 sc in next st, do not join (34 sts).

Fasten off, leaving a 36"/91.4cm tail. Make invisible join as illustrated on page 8. Do not weave in end. Instead use it to whipstitch one sole onto each leg, making sure to line up corners of 3 hdcs. Whipstitch the sole of the foot into rnd 32 of the leg, leaving the entire sl st exposed. Stuff the foot, making sure as you do this that there is enough stuffing in the leg and that the corners at the front of the feet are filled out.

To make knees, sew a dent back and forth across the front of each leg with a short length of color A, stitching between rnds 10 and 11, five posts apart. Tie in a tight knot, and weave in ends.

Cut two 18"/45.7cm lengths of color E, and, using photo as a guide, use satin stitch to embroider lines for flip-flop thongs. Weave in ends.

## Tail (make 1)

*Note:* Tail is worked in a continuous spiral. Do not join rnds. You may wish to use a marker to indicate the beginning of the rnd.

Stuff the tail with fiberfill as you crochet. Working the stuffing down to the very tip can be tricky.

Starting at tip, with 3.25mm/D-3 hook and color A, mr.

**Rnd 1:** Ch 1, work 6 sc in ring; do not join, pull starting ring closed (6 sc).

**Rnd 2:** 2 sc in each sc around (12 sc).

**Rnd 3:** Sc around, invdec once (11 sts).

**Rnds 4–7:** Sc in each sc.

**Rnds 8–22:** Rep rnds 3–7 three times; avoid placing decreases in the same place on each rnd (8 sts at end of rnd 19).

**Rnds 23–32:** Sc in each sc around.

Fasten off, leaving an 18"/45.7cm yarn tail for sewing the monkey's tail to the body. Stuff the tail with fiberfill. Pin tail to body through the hole in the shorts and sew in place. Weave in ends.

Pinch the shorts together between the legs. Sew closed with a short length of color D.

## Star Appliqué

Cut a star out of felt using the template on page 63 as a guide.

Embroider blanket stitch around the edge using the Perle cotton and embroidery needle. Glue the star to the monkey's T-shirt, using straight pins to keep it in place while it dries.

This project was made with 1 skein each of

**Color A:** Caron's Simply Soft Brites (100% acrylic, 3.5oz/100g, 166yd/152m), in #2609, Berry Blue

**Color B:** Caron's Simply Soft Brites (100% acrylic, 3.5oz/100g, 166yd/152m), in #2607, Limelight

**Color C:** Red Heart's Soft (100% acrylic, 5oz/140g, approx 256yd/234m), in #5142, Cherry Red

**Color D:** Caron's Simply Soft (100% acrylic, 3.5oz/100g, 166 yd/152 m), in #2713, Buttercup

**Color E:** Caron's Simply Soft (100% acrylic, 3.5oz/100g, 166 yd/152 m), in #2680, Black

# Templates

All 100%

Piglet, page 43
Front Feet

Piglet, page 43
Rear Feet

Werner the Wiener Dog,
page 36

Outer

Inner

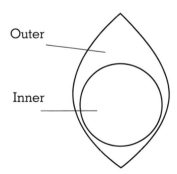

Friends Forever Fawn,
page 49

Benny the Monkey, page 55

Fresh Strawberries, page 18

## Author Bio

Elisabeth Doherty received her B.A. in Fine Art from Columbia College in Chicago with the intention of making serious paintings about serious subjects. It turned out she was better at making toys. This unexpected path offered an unexpected bonus: it helped her maintain her mental health. Fortunately, enough people like the things she makes, so that galleries keep asking her to send them things and crafters keep asking her to write down her patterns. Please visit her website at www.gourmetamigurumi.com.

## Others in the Simply Series